THE CURIOUS
BARISTA'S
Guide to

COFFEE

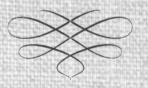

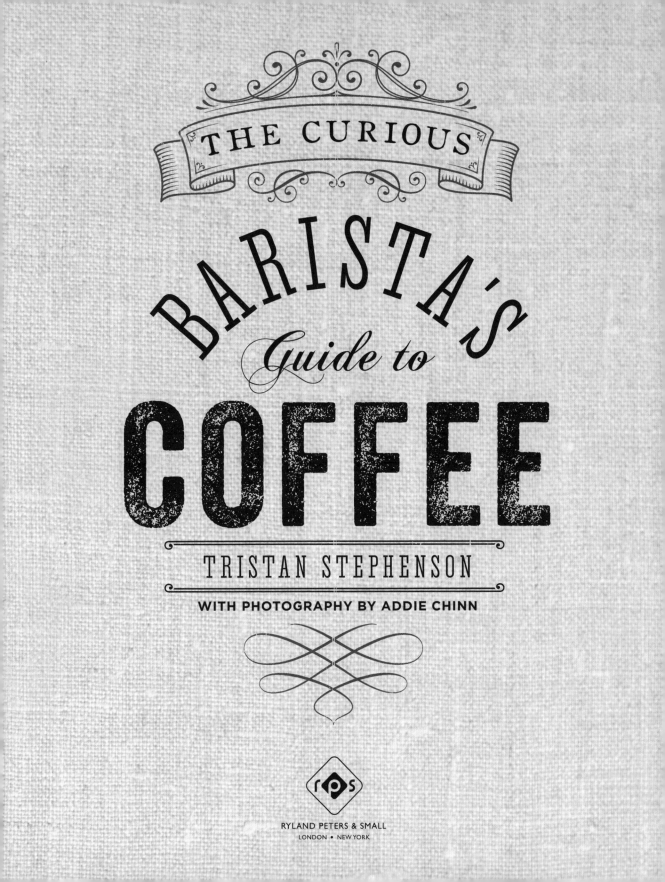

THE CURIOUS

BARISTA'S
Guide to
COFFEE

TRISTAN STEPHENSON

WITH PHOTOGRAPHY BY ADDIE CHINN

RYLAND PETERS & SMALL
LONDON • NEW YORK

Designer Geoff Borin
Commissioning Editor Nathan Joyce
Production Manager Gordana Simakovic
Art Director Leslie Harrington
Editorial Director Julia Charles
Publisher Cindy Richards

Prop Stylist Sarianne Plaisant
Indexer Vanessa Bird

First published in 2015 by
Ryland Peters & Small
20–21 Jockey's Fields
London WC1R 4BW
and
341 East 116th Street
New York, NY 10029

www.rylandpeters.com

10 9 8 7 6 5 4 3

Text © Tristan Stephenson 2015

Design and commissioned photographs
© Ryland Peters & Small 2015

See page 192 for full photographic credits.

ISBN: 978-1-84975-563-4

A CIP record for this book is available
from the British Library.

US Library of Congress CIP data has been
applied for.

Printed in China

Note: the metric system is often favoured
by coffee enthusiasts because it is more
accurate when it comes to precision
measurement, but imperial measurements
are also provided in this book. Purchasing
a set of digital scales is recommended to
ensure accuracy.

CONTENTS

INTRODUCTION

For a lot of people, a cup of coffee need only be something of passable quality and sufficient heat that delivers the expected caffeine kick. The daily grind of life becomes a more evenly matched contest when there's a mug of coffee at your side or a paper cup of it in your hand. I can't deny that I've enjoyed the energizing effects of caffeine, and it's certainly questionable whether this book would have been completed without it!

The adoption of Italian espresso culture over the past 60 years has awarded the humble cup of joe with a refreshing new makeover, transforming coffee into something evocative, aspirational and sexy, while at the same time asking even the most macho of men to embrace fashionable Continental terms like 'macchiato'. The espresso bar has, in turn, paved the way for the rise of the now ubiquitous American style chain-café which, these days, stands as a cultural middle ground between home and work, relaxation and concentration, comfort and functionality... oh, and they sell coffee, too.

We are now seeing a new wave of quality-focused coffee shops that aim to pique our curiosity and satisfy our desire for a delicious drink, and, for a growing number of people, a good coffee is becoming much more than a simple agent of stimulation. We are beginning to recognize that coffee can contain a wealth of appreciable and sometimes unexpected flavours, but also that those who make good coffee are worthy of the same degree of recognition that any other complex culinary field would warrant. These baristas carry an air of quiet erudition about them as the new breed of coffee shop aspires to engage its customers in earnest dialogue over such things as coffee origin, roast style and brewing method.

The plethora of flavours and aromas that a cup of coffee can offer has, in turn, inspired us to dig deeper, and we are beginning to discover the fact that a great cup of coffee has a story behind it, too. The history of coffee's ascent to prominence is part of that, but also the physical journey of a cup of coffee and the concerted efforts of numerous people across various parts of the world. Recognizing the fragility of this journey, coupled with the occasional glimpses of liquid perfection as every element comes together, is what makes some of these moments exploring coffee very special indeed.

We live in a time where our raw and roasted coffee has never tasted better, and the individuals who are driving its quality and success forward have never been more empowered. The coffee trade is more transparent than ever and delicious speciality coffee is easily obtainable. This book explores how coffee has reached this stage of development, the processes that it takes to get to us, why it tastes the way it does, and the considerations and practices that go into brewing amazing coffee drinks.

HOW TO USE THIS BOOK

The first section of this book documents coffee's extraordinary history. It's fair to say that coffee has influenced the world we live in, having played its part in politics, economics, philosophy and technology for over 500 years and continuing to fuel the thoughts of the great thinkers of the modern era. Books like this one only exist as a result of the things that have come before, and when writing this book I found myself taking time out from all the scientific geekery of brewing delicious drinks, and grounding myself in a piece of history from coffee's turbulent past.

The next chunk of the book covers all things concerning the production of coffee. This takes us from tropical farms, through to the processing of coffee cherries and on to the multifarious art of coffee roasting. All the stages of coffee production are necessary practical steps towards creating a physical cup of coffee, but within that they each harbour idiosyncrasies in the form of practices or methods, derived either from trial and error or tradition, which through scientific understanding can now be manipulated and exploited to great

effect. Each of these factors combines and culminates in the coffee that you're sipping on now, whether it's a sad and lifeless cup of instant or the finest speciality coffee brewed to perfection. In this section, I also endeavour to explore some of the science of coffee flavour, while looking into such things as caffeine, water and the physics and chemistry of extracting flavour from ground coffee.

The following part of the book is about grinding and brewing (the latter is split into three chapters: espresso, espresso-based drinks and other brewing methods). We start with the different grind sizes and the impact on the resulting cup of coffee. From there, we move on to the vast array of brewing paraphernalia available to the modern barista, each unique in its approach towards separating brewed coffee from spent coffee grounds, and each unique in its ability to cast light on the numerous contours of coffee's character.

The final section in the main part of the book includes a range of coffee-based drinks that I have developed over the years. Some are original creations, and others are based on food and drink that you are very likely familiar with – albeit with a twist. These recipes are diverse, but the one thing that they have in common is the celebration of coffee flavour.

At the rear of the book, I've included an appendix, split into two parts. The first is an exploration of 40 coffee-producing countries, with a concise description of their respective histories, the size of their operations and the style and quality of some of their most exciting coffees. The second part focuses on a dozen different varieties of coffee, along with their respective features and merits. Just like grapes in wine, specific varieties produce a range of different-looking coffee beans that go on to produce quite different-tasting cups of coffee.

Koffi-boom

THE HISTORY AND ORIGINS OF COFFEE

Just like the human race, coffee's origins can be traced to Ethiopia. Who'd have thought that the legendary discovery of a humble goatherder would have gone on to lead to the formation of nations, revolutions and pioneering scientific inventions. Don't believe me? Pour yourself a cup and read on...

It may be pure chance that coffee arrived in what we know now as the Middle East at the dawn of an unprecedented period of learning and enlightenment in the 9th and 10th centuries. It could also be a coincidence that in the 1,000 years that followed, on more than a few occasions, the cultural discovery of coffee preceded a sharp ascent to global power: from Ottoman, to British, French, Spanish, Portuguese, Dutch and American.

It's probably also a coincidence that coffee-drinking establishments have, time, and time again, fertilized new ways of thinking, challenged class systems and fostered learning and debate. Indeed, some of the greatest names in history lived in a space and time surrounded by coffee-drinking culture, and sipped on more than a few cups themselves – from Isaac Newton, to Beethoven, Napoleon and even Steve Jobs. In some instances, the influence of coffee and coffee houses has sparked some of history's most significant revolutions, civil wars and uprisings. Coincidence perhaps, but plausible enough that religious leaders, kings and politicians have smelled the coffee, pointed the finger, and in some cases even banned the bean altogether.

Coffee has only been consumed in Europe in the last four centuries. It only crossed the Atlantic to the New World a mere 300 years ago. And yet, in that time, it has been responsible for the formation of nations, the perpetuation of slavery, the creation of media platforms and the incarnation of massive trading conglomerates, and established financial institutions that are intrinsic to our global economic infrastructure. Its legacy has seeped into many aspects of our lives, not least politics, journalism, science and literature.

WHERE IT ALL BEGAN

Our journey begins in Ethiopia. While it is generally accepted that Ethiopia is the birthplace of coffee, it's quite likely that it was simply the first place that the crop truly flourished after spreading from the Sudan. Exactly when its leaves, cherries, or beans were first consumed is a mystery, though. What we do know is that around 2,000 years ago, the nomadic Oromos tribe, living in the kingdom of Kefa (in modern-day Ethiopia), were known to have moulded the leaves and fruit of the coffee tree into a kind of cake that could be sucked and chewed on – rather like a caffeinated chewing gum – giving them a temporary boost of energy. Later evidence is rather circumstantial, however. In the 5th century AD, the Kingdom of Aksum ruled northern Ethiopia and parts of southern Egypt, and at this time, Aksum was doing a roaring trade with the Roman Empire, but, alas, there's no record of a Roman ever drinking a cup of coffee...

It's possible that coffee was planted in the kingdom of Himyar (now part of modern-day Yemen) shortly after the Kingdom of Aksum had invaded. Failing that, the 7th century saw plenty more interaction between the people of Ethiopia and Yemen, on both a political and intellectual level. It also saw the rise of Islam – much to coffee's benefit. Some time later, the Arab trading routes from Yemen, namely the port of Mokha, became responsible for coffee's domination of the Middle East.

The legendary tale of coffee's discovery is worthy of a mention, though. The story goes that it was first discovered by a young Ethiopian goatherder called Kaldi. This story, more than any other, has stuck because it's cute, vaguely believable, and open to a touch of embellishment. Kaldi was tending to his herd one evening when he noticed that they exhibited a certain friskiness after nibbling on the leaves and red cherries of a particular tree. Confused, and a more than a little intrigued, Kaldi tried the fruit for himself. The effect was almost immediate – he felt energized, motivated and alert. Kaldi had discovered caffeine, the most widely consumed drug in the world today. What happened next is open to debate; some say Kaldi took the fruit and leaves to elders, or religious men nearby, while others say that the influence of coffee made Kaldi rather 'attached' to his herd.

In time, Yemen developed its own story of the discovery of coffee, which tells a tale of a man called Omar who was condemned to die outside Mokha's city walls. During his wanderings in the wilderness, Omar found a coffee tree and ate its fruit, which gave him the energy he required to return to the city. His survival was seen as a blessing, and so too was the discovery of the coffee plant, which subsequently became the beverage of choice for the residents of Mokha. The Arabs called the drink *qwaha* (the Arab word for wine), and since Muslims are forbidden to drink alcohol, coffee was probably about as close as they were likely to get to a bottle of plonk.

ARABIAN AND OTTOMAN COFFEE

Coffee spread with Islam, as it was commonly used in the performance of religious ceremonies to assist with all-night prayer sessions. It was probably at some point during this time, while Europe was wallowing in the Dark Ages, that the seeds (beans) of the coffee plant were first dried, roasted and ground up to make the first cup recognizable by today's standards.

Coffee became an important trading commodity for Arab nations, with the world's first coffee houses probably popping up in Yemen by the end of the 15th century. But following a trend that was destined to repeat itself, some leaders took a disliking to the stimulation that coffee granted their subjects. In 1511, Mecca's governor, Kha'ir Beg, presented a pot of coffee to a council of legal experts and literally put it on trial for purportedly 'making people drunk, or at least dispos'd them to commit disorders forbidden by the Law'. He was successful, too – coffee was burned

ABOVE A 19th-century painting of three noblewomen (and a child) enjoying a pot of coffee in one of Bethlehem's coffee houses.

in the streets and coffee houses were forced to cease trading the drink. The ruling was revoked only a few months later, by orders from higher up the chain of command, but over the following 200 years, similar decrees were made, then subsequently revoked, by sultans, governors, kings and authorities of other Arab regions and beyond.

Once the Ottoman Turks took control of Yemen in 1517, they recognized how valuable a commodity coffee was, and passed strict laws on how coffee was exported, the aim being to reduce the risk of coffee being grown anywhere outside of Yemen. Coffee cherries had to be first steeped in boiling water, or partially roasted before being shipped to Suez, then overland to Alexandria for trading with European ports. This worked for a while, but inevitably someone managed to sneak some seeds out (by taping them to his stomach, so the story goes) and they were successfully cultivated in India.

There were mentions of coffee in European literature towards the end of the 16th century, and the first illustration of the plant appeared in Prosper Alpin's *Book of Egyptian Plants* (1592). Alpin even mused that the Turks used the berries to make a 'decoction or drinke'. Further interest in the exotic plant and the Turkish drink that it made was recounted by the Dutch physician known as Paludanus in his *Itinerario* (1596):

'This drinke they take every morning fasting in their chambers, out of an earthen pot, being verie hote [...] and they say it strengtheneth and maketh them warme, breaketh wind, and openeth any stopping.'

In 1610 Constantinople (present day Istanbul), the gem in the crown of the Ottoman empire, was the largest and richest city in the world. At the time, the most popular drink was called Coffa, 'black as soote, and tasting not much unlike it'. The strange practices of the powerful Ottoman empire piqued the curiosity of the Europeans. Here, after all, was one of the largest empires that had ever existed, stretching from Northern Africa to Eastern Europe, and at the height of its power right up to the gates of Vienna. The Coffa plant and its fruit became a subject of great interest for European botanists and physicians, but the benefits of drinking coffee piqued the curiosity of nearly everyone.

BELOW Coffee has always been a social drink, as this 1870 illustration of an Arabian coffee house portrays.

THE RISE OF THE COFFEE HOUSE

By the early 1600s, the coffee bean had made its way to British shores and in 1652 the first European coffee house opened in London. Pasqua Rosee's coffee house was actually more of a stall, located in the churchyard of St Michael's, just off London's bustling Cornhill. Rosee was thought to have been born early in the 17th century in Sicily. A shrewd businessman, he teamed up with Christopher Bowman, a freeman of the City of London, in order to appease the resistance of local alehouse owners to an outsider. The store was a big hit, and as the benefits of this magical drink became apparent ('good after-relish' and 'breaking of wind in abundance' were two ways that it was described) the stall soon became a large house, as it relocated across the road.

Coffee shops popped up in London like toadstools in the night. A mere ten years after Rosee's shop served its first cup, there were thought to be nearly 100 'coffee men' in London, with coffee houses also opening in Oxford and Cambridge. By the turn of the 18th century, some estimated the number at more than 1,000.

Coffee was the great soberer in a time where breakfast consisted of a small beer and when two pennies would get you extremely drunk. It was the antidote to alcohol's generally debilitating effects, including the numbing of the senses and propensity to lead to toxic daytime brawls. This Turkish drink stimulated the mind, provoked discussion, ritualized debate, and encouraged rational enquiry on all manner of topics between like-minded people. As one anonymous English poem from 1674 put it, coffee was, '...that grave and wholesome liquor, that heals the stomach, makes the Genius quicker, Relieves the memory, revives the sad, and cheers the spirits, without making mad.'

Seats could not be reserved in a coffee house, there were no class prejudices, and besides women no one would be refused entrance. Here, merchants, politicians, lobbyists, intellectuals, scientists, journalists, scholars, poets and common men alike all took seats, sometimes to discuss business, but most of the time simply to enjoy a coffee and partake in the discourse and debate of their chosen subject, all to the 'rattling noise of Kettle, Skimmers and Ladles among the Braziers'.

John Starky's *A Character of Coffee and Coffee-Houses* (1661) eloquently summarizes the situation:

'Here is no respect of persons. Boldly therefor let any person, who comes to drink Coffee sit down in the very Chair, for here a Seat is to be given to no man. That great privilege of equality is only peculiar to the Golden Age, and to a Coffee-house.'

Coffee houses were ideal places to chew the political fat, too, which could, and probably did, include talk of dissent and treason. Charles II (1660–85) of England placed spies in the London's coffee shops then attempted to ban the establishments altogether, claiming in a proclamation issued on 29th December 1675 that they caused men to, 'mis-spend much of their time, which might and probably would otherwise by imployed in and about their Lawful Callings and Affairs.' The bill was never

ABOVE The interior of an early London coffee house shows a room that is buzzing with activity.

passed, however, thanks to appeals from coffee men and politicians alike.

By the end of the 17th century, some London coffee shops had started to become referred to as 'penny universities'. They became a breeding ground for new ways of scientific thinking, an incubator for hypotheses and theories, and sometimes even a staging ground for what were termed 'natural philosophy' demonstrations and experiments.

Since many coffee houses specialized in specific fields of business, news, arts, discussion or learning, it was shops such as the Grecian, Marine and Garraways that the likes of Christopher Wren (the architect of St. Paul's Cathedral) and the English scientist Robert Hooke would visit. The Marine also became the stage for James Hodgson, one of London's earliest celebrity scientists. Isaac Newton's eponymous work, *Principia*, in which he shared his gravity theory for the first time, was published in 1687, and some would say, had more to do with his local Cambridge coffee house than it did with fallen apples.

The Scottish academic Adam Smith wrote a large part of what is perhaps the most important piece of literature concerning economics and finance of any time – *The Wealth of Nations* – in the British Coffee Shop in London. Coffee houses like the British Coffee Shop functioned as common rooms in which to discuss the topics of trade and commerce, where a network of runners could rapidly disseminate

stock-sensitive news from the colonies among all the relevant coffee shops. Jonathan's coffee shop was one such coffee hangout that became a popular alternative trading post to the Royal Exchange when strict protocols were enforced by the crown. Almost 100 years later, in 1773, a group of traders broke away and established a new coffee shop, called New Jonathan's. That name lasted only a short time, however, and it became known as the Stock Exchange (now known as the London Stock Exchange).

One of the world's largest insurance brokers, Lloyds of London, also started life as a coffee shop, and even today the porters who work there are referred to as waiters. Well-known publications such as *The Spectator*, *The Guardian* and *Tatler* were either directly birthed from or heavily influenced by the coffee shop, too. News and commentary that would previously have only been the preserve of the higher social ranks was suddenly available to the masses. *Tatler*, when it first launched in 1709, even had section headers named after prominent London coffee shops.

And what of the coffee itself? Not so good, it seems. In his 1661 book, *A Character of Coffee and Coffee Houses*, John Starky colourfully describes the drinks he received with such phrases as 'boiled soot', 'made with the scent of old crusts', and I have seen other references to 'horse pond liquor', and 'hot hell-broth'. Most coffee houses roasted their own, of course, and given the above descriptions it is fair to say they may have been on the darker side, but it's likely that questionable brewing methods, adopted from Ottoman practices, where coffee is repeatedly boiled, is the cause for the strongly brewed and bitter brews that most shops served. Some 17th-century recipes even recommended using water that has been

previously boiled for 15 minutes with old coffee grounds to season it. The appearance of the drink perhaps took greater precedence over its flavour and some shop owners experimented with elaborate filtration techniques, using egg whites and isinglass (a substance extracted from the swim bladders of fish) in an attempt to clarify their brews and remove some of the sludge. It was also commonplace to brew all the coffee in the morning, then reheat it to order throughout the day, which is another practice that would have done no favour for the flavour.

Paris' first coffee house opened in 1672, 20 years after London, with some sources even suggesting that the our old friend Pasqua Rosée was involved in its conception. Virtually all traces of its existence appear to have been lost to time, unfortunately. This contrasts with Café Procope, which was established in 1686, and became a famous meeting place of the French Enlightenment; Rousseau, Diderot and Voltaire frequented it. Indeed, Voltaire, who was rumoured to have consumed 40 cups of coffee a day, arguably conceived his *Encyclopédie*, the world's first modern encyclopedia at Café Procope. Two of America's founding fathers, Thomas Jefferson and Benjamin Franklin, were also known to meet at Café Procope, which still exists today, incidentally.

Another popular Parisian coffee house, Café de Foy, was the stage for the rallying cry that started the French Revolution. Under the watchful eyes of police spies, while standing on a table brandishing a pistol, Camille Desmoulins roused his countrymen with his historic appeal '*Aux armes, citoyens!*' on 12th July 1789. The Bastille fell two days later, and the French Revolution had begun.

Although it was irrefutably London that was hit hardest by the coffee-house bug, most European cities had at least one coffee house by the close of the 1670s and the first American shop was opened in Boston in 1671. New York had to wait another 25 years to get its first, which was opened by a British immigrant on South Broadway.

THE DRINK OF THE NEW WORLD

At the beginning of the 18th century, coffee consumption in Europe was higher than it have ever been and European nations were becoming increasingly nervous about their reliance on coffee shipped from Mokha through the trading port of Venice. The Dutch were the first to take action when they successfully cultivated seedlings in India's Malabar region and in Dutch Ceylon (Sri Lanka), and then in 1699 took some seedlings to Batavia (the former name of the present-day capital, Jakarta) in Java. Around a decade later, 360 kg/800 lbs of Dutch-grown Java coffee arrived in Amsterdam and sold for a very high price. The Arab monopoly on coffee had been broken, and before too long, the Dutch megacorporation known as the VOC (Vereenigde Oost-Indische Compagnie), was shipping over half of all the coffee consumed in Europe from its colonial ports in Java, a city that would forever be synonymous with coffee.

Around the same time that the Dutch began growing coffee in Indonesia the French took small trees to the island of Bourbon (now known as Réunion), which lies 800 km/500 miles east of Madagascar, in the Indian Ocean. Some reports suggest that these trees came from Java, while others suggest that they were a gift from a Yemeni Sultan; other reports even claim that coffee was indigenous to the island. However it got there, it was a pivotal moment in the development of coffee as we know it today, because the tree mutated into a new variety that later became known as bourbon.

Bourbon varieties produce around 20 per cent more fruit than typical varieties (see page 24), and when one French official visited Bourbon in 1711 he

BELOW Gabriel de Clieu famously sharing water rations with his precious coffee sapling during the long voyage across the Atlantic in 1720.

found 'wild coffee trees, of a height of ten to twelve feet, fill of fruit'. It took another 150 years before the variety was planted in Brazil, but thanks to the clean acidity and balance that bourbon varieties exhibited – of which there are now nearly two dozen including mutations and hybrids – they are among the most highly respected in the world today.

The Netherlands was also probably the first nation to cultivate coffee in the West Indies, having sent plants to its Surinam colony in the Guianas (in north-eastern South America) as early as 1713. The more popular legend of coffee's arrival in the Americas occurred seven years later, however, in 1720, when Gabriel de Clieu, a captain in the French navy, transported a single coffee plant across the Atlantic. The story of the escapade is detailed in his personal account, *Année littéraire*, published in 1774. If de Clieu is to believed (or even if not, for that matter) then Hollywood is surely missing a trick, as it turns out to be a tale of blockbuster proportions.

De Clieu correctly determined that coffee would grow just fine in any region where sugarcane flourished, so the French island of Martinique was a sure bet. However, our hero didn't own a coffee plant himself and would first need to acquire one. The slight hitch was that at the time there was only one known example in all of France – a gift from the Mayor of Amsterdam to King Louis XIV – and it was contained within the greenhouses of the French royal gardens. De Clieu used his good looks and charm to seduce a local 'lady of good quality' and persuaded her to court one of the royal physicians. His arm sufficiently twisted, the physician stole the plant from the greenhouse and gave it to de Clieu.

Wasting no time, de Clieu secreted himself and his prize (safely contained within a terrarium of his own making) aboard a French navy ship destined for Martinique. What perils genuinely befell him will remain a mystery, but according to his account he safeguarded his plant through storms, attack by Tunisian pirates, attempted theft by a Dutch spy (who apparently manage to rip a few leaves off the plant), starvation, sea monsters, and much more besides. For some weeks during the voyage, the rationing of drinking water was in effect and de Clieu was even forced to share his ration with his beloved sapling. None of it was in vain, though, as de Clieu successfully planted the tree on Martinique and seeded new plants. The numbers vary wildly, but one count of coffee trees on the island a mere nine years later totalled around 3 million.

Following the success on Martinique, other French islands took cuttings or were gifted coffee seedlings. Coffee plantations around the Caribbean and central America grew at an exponential rate. Coffee hit Colombia in 1723, Brazil in 1727 – allegedly smuggled in a bouquet of flowers that was gifted from the wife of the governor of French Guyana to a Brazilian lieutenant-colonel – Jamaica in 1728, Venezuela in 1730, Hispaniola (present-day Dominican Republic and Haiti) in 1735, Guatemala in 1747 and Cuba in 1748.

By 1780, San Domingo in Haiti provided no less than half of the world's supply of coffee. Virtually all the coffee in the Americas, and indeed nearly all the coffee in commercial production at the time, could trace its lineage to a single tree planted in the conservatory of King Louis XIV in 1713.

GLOBAL DOMINATION

The development of sugar beet as an alternative to sugarcane in the early 1800s caused the price of that most reliable of new world crops to plummet. Demand for coffee in Europe remained on the increase, however, so many of the colonies in Central and South America ramped up production and provided a ready supply of green beans. If the events of the Boston Tea Party on 6th December 1773 wasn't enough to get America drinking coffee, the War of 1812, which temporarily cut off tea shipments as well as seeing America adopt all things French, including coffee, was enough to secure coffee as the national drink.

No one gained more from this than Brazil, where coffee was seen less as agriculture and more as industry – an approach that remains largely in place even today. Huge swathes of land in the Paraíba River area, near the city of Rio de Janeiro, were swallowed up to coffee plantations, employing the efforts of entire legions of slaves and lining the pockets of the super-rich coffee barons. By 1920, Brazil claimed up to 80 per cent of the world's coffee supply; today it is around 35 per cent.

Unfortunately the themes of slavery, inequality and capitalism were not unique to Brazilian coffee history. The passage of this black gold through the 19th and 20th centuries sees, time and time again, the interference of the Europeans and later on the Americans, who leveraged their economic might to quietly manipulate or brashly and unashamedly bend a coffee-producing nation to their will. For many of these countries, coffee became a ball and chain that bridled them in their early developmental stages, and served only to fulfil the needs of wealthy western nations. In many African coffee-producing countries, colonialism, mostly under the British and Belgians, crippled and constricted development. The likes of Kenya and Malawi had no ownership or control over their farms, but things were even worse in Burundi where, in 1933, every farmer in the Belgian- controlled central African nation was forced to grow a minimum of 50 coffee trees.

Even when decolonization began after World War II, many of the world's coffee-producing countries continued to struggle through civil uprising, social upheaval, economic depression, political instability and foreign trade embargoes, not to mention coffee leaf rust (see page 28), coffee market instability and drought. And in far too many cases the newly installed governments of these damaged nations were no better than the ones that had come before. The stories of such acts make for depressing reading, such as the indigenous families of Guatemala who were displaced from their land to make way for coffee plantations, or the indigo farmers of El Salvador who received little or no compensation when their smallholdings were seized by the state to grow coffee.

It wasn't all doom and gloom, of course, but squeaky-clean success stories are few and far between. In Central America, it is Costa Rica that stands as the pin-up coffee nation, and this is partly thanks to a government that has, for almost 200 years, gently encouraged its citizens to grow coffee – at one time they even gave away coffee seeds and land for free!

In general, the 20th century saw a continuous rise in demand for coffee. Coffee consumption in the US grew more or less every year, reaching a peak in 1946, when the average American was consuming nearly 1 kg/2.2 lbs a month – twice that of the figures for 1900. The popularity of instant soluble coffee has increased American imports, and this in turn drove the market for cheaper robusta coffee (see page 24), which has helped put coffee-producing countries like Vietnam on the map.

Prior to the introduction of instant coffee, the past 200 years has seen the dynamic between green coffee and the consumer change significantly. Coffee began as an exotic drink that was served to people who visited coffee houses, before evolving into something that was both roasted and brewed in the family home. The shift to buying pre-roasted coffee took much longer than it probably should have and this was largely down to (quite rightly) consumer fear about shady counterfeit coffee, made from chicory, peas, corn... pretty much anything. An important law was passed in Germany in 1875 that forbade the sale of 'substitute' coffee beans marketed as coffee. Counterfeit and adulterated coffee had been blighting the German market for some time, with one journal for housewives, published in 1845, advising women to wash their

In cool, dewy shade—under an awning of taller trees—these fine coffee beans in their gay red jackets
slowly store up the rich "shade-grown" flavor that America loves in Chase & Sanborn Coffee.

"Shade-Grown" Flavor

CHASE &
SANBORN
COFFEE

EXPLAINS WHY MORE PEOPLE HAVE BEEN USING
CHASE & SANBORN COFFEE IN THE PAST YEAR THAN EVER BEFORE!

IN coffee, "shade-grown" means *slow*-grown. It means *mellow*-grown. It means *flavor*-grown.

Shade allows the good earth of the tropics to work slowly and completely in creating this heavenly flavor.

This is the "shade-grown" flavor that adds so much to the Chase & Sanborn blend. No wonder Chase & Sanborn tastes so mellow...so smooth...so rich!

No wonder more people have been using Chase & Sanborn Coffee in the past year than ever before!

No wonder that each day hundreds of families fall in love with Chase & Sanborn's "shade-grown" flavor!

coffee beans before grinding to check if ink leaches out. The new legislation did great things for consumer faith in off-the-shelf roasted coffee though, rapidly killing off the home-roasting tradition, while hugely increasing demand for commercially roasted coffee.

It might seem hypocritical to celebrate the death of home roasting in a book that teaches you how to roast at home (see pages 58–59) but I think it goes without saying that things have moved on since then. It's important to note, though, that Germany was perhaps more ahead of the time that any other nation in creating a stable commercial coffee roasting industry with quality at its core, which goes some way towards explaining why German coffee roasters are the most sought after.

THE EVOLUTION OF THE CAFÉ

For most of the world it has been the rise of espresso drinking culture that has driven coffee consumption outside of the home over the past 50 years. In Europe, the Italians did an exceptional job of arousing a sense of romance and passion in us when it comes to the no-longer-so-simple act of drinking a cup of coffee. Espresso bars first appeared in the 1950s, in London, Melbourne, Wellington and San Francisco, and were initially perceived by many as fake, showy, overly-stylized and downright weird. The sociologist, Richard Hobbart described that atmosphere of one London espresso bar in 1957 as 'spiritual dry-rot amid the odour of boiled milk'. Those that frequented such establishments tended to be of the younger generation and were labelled by their elders as 'wild, sexually promiscuous and irresponsible' – although this seems a common complaint between one generation and the next. It seems plausible to me that those who were embracing the espresso bar were experiencing a taste of not just a new type of coffee, but also of the enlightenment and liberation that had been granted to those who frequented the coffee houses of the 17th century.

Over the decades that followed, the knee-jerk reaction that had initially fought to culturally fend-

off the espresso bar slackened into an embrace, as all things Continental became a badge of honour. The espresso machine became an icon of modernity in its time, and remains a powerful statement of well-cultured taste even today.

But the truly authentic espresso bar, as Continentally quintessential as it may sound – where a 60-second visit grants one enough time to order, demolish, and pay for a drink without even taking a seat – has never truly found traction outside of Italy. It has been softened and adapted to meet the standards of the working-class man, business executive and lady who lunches (among many others) alike. In many respects the Italian roots of espresso have paled over the past 20 years, only to be replaced by a new style of coffee appreciation that, rather alarmingly, has little to do with actual coffee (although they would have you believe otherwise).

Growth of the American-style coffee chain, born out of the West Coast anti-establishment and whole-food movement of the late 1960s, still pushes on, and the likes of Starbucks now adorn not only the towns and cities of the western world, but the rest of the world, too. The commercialization of 'milk and sugar coffee' has in fact reached such a point of ubiquity that, some would say, the cities of our world are quickly becoming carbon copies of one another, with the same inescapable shop fronts (and café interiors) wherever you go – ironic, given the motivations behind their humble origins.

This kind of success doesn't come without being popular, however, which means that, for many of us, the prevalence of such places is a positive thing. The most obvious reason for this is the function that they serve as a 'third place' between work and home: one which is reliable, unchanging and accessible wherever you are. While some of the individuality may be lost in these chains, in many respects they are the same as those of the 17th century, acutely aware of and cleverly balancing the dual purpose of being both a place that coffee can be enjoyed and somewhere where higher cultural values can be appreciated. Think about it: a seat in Starbucks grants one access to a forum for any kind of discussion, limitless creative space, research tools for the sciences and arts, media libraries and cutting edge news – all you need is a laptop and a WiFi password. Coffee is optional, as the Starbucks' logo would attest to; once proudly stating 'Starbucks Coffee', it now makes no mention coffee at all.

One major development of the past 20 years is how discerning in our ordering rituals we have become. The element of choice in a café has become a expressive device with which we can communicate personal taste and product understanding in an otherwise homogenized high-street environment. The coffee menu at a typical chain store offers maybe six varieties of drink, four types of milk, two or three espresso sizes, half-a-dozen flavoured sauces and three beverage sizes, totalling well over 1,000 different permutations. The trick is in the demystifying design of the menu, which seeks to process and output our order as rapidly as possible. Of course our decision is more often made before we even walk in, but even when some deliberation occurs, it is surprising how rapidly we can trim 1,000 options down to a single order.

And now it is the notion of removing choice – which only a short time ago was celebrated by the world's best cafés – that defines the new wave of quality-driven hipster hangouts. In these minimalist inner-city sanctuaries, we see the counter-culture movement once again partnering with coffee, where quality, knowledge and attention to detail are the overriding themes (sometimes at the sacrifice of good service) and excellent coffee the backbone. Many of these cafés hold their product in such high regard that they will roast their own coffee, directing consumer decision-making specifically to the brew method and the origin and processing method of the coffee. In most instances, it is expertise of the barista in which we place our trust, which broadens the dynamic further. In this way the entire concept of a cup of coffee evolves from being an indulgent treat, caffeinated pick-me-up or expression of individuality, into a beverage that contains all the nuance and refinement of a fine wine or gourmet steak, naturally drawing attention to our apparent appreciation of such things in the action of drinking it.

Where cafés will go next is difficult to say, but it will no doubt be beneficial to everyone. Certainly it would appear that the large chains are becoming increasingly influenced by the focus on provenance and traceability of the smaller, craft-focused independents; improvements among the large chains in the areas of training and quality should follow. If I were putting my neck on the line, I would argue that many of the independents could learn a lot from the customer service standards of some of the chains, especially in the US. Some cutting-edge coffee shops have succumbed to a certain elitist attitude, validated by their belief in their own superiority through the acquisition of coffee knowledge, which can come across stand-offish – 'You want the golden-honey pacamara brewed in siphon?!' – or just plain rude. I hope to see this weeded out in the coming years.

RIGHT Craft, transparency and skinny jeans are the three pillars that support the new wave of cafés.

GROWING, HARVESTING AND PROCESSING COFFEE

02

SPECIES AND VARIETIES

Coffee grows on trees – coffee trees. It may seem like an obvious distinction, but one that is worth making. All coffee trees belong to the *Rubiaceae* family of flowering plants, and more specifically, the *Coffea* genus, which currently encompasses over 120 individual species of plant, ranging from small shrubs to 18-m/60-ft high trees. *Coffea* species grow wild across various parts of the tropics and new species continue to be discovered. Strictly speaking, only two species of the *Coffea* genus are actually cultivated for coffee production: *Coffea Arabica* (arabica) and *Coffea Canephora* (commonly referred to as 'robusta'), but there are a handful of countries, such as the Philippines, that grow small amounts of a third species, *Coffea Liberica*, for domestic consumption.

Around 70 per cent of the world's commercially grown coffee are varieties of arabica, which adds up to about 7 million tons of roasted coffee every year. The rest grow robusta, most of which comes from India, the Indonesian islands of Java and Sumatra, and Vietnam, the latter of which produces nearly half of all the world's total output of robusta coffee and is the second-biggest coffee grower after Brazil.

As the name suggests, robusta is the more disease-resistant of the two main species, and this is in part due to its higher caffeine content, which acts as a deterrent to small pests. Robusta typically yields comparatively more fruit per harvest, plus its ripe fruit hangs on the tree and withers, unlike arabica, which must be picked before it falls onto the ground. Robusta produces a smaller and less elongated bean than arabica, and it generally possesses a stronger, albeit less desirable flavour. It's for this reason that robusta is often used as a small part of espresso blends, prized by the Italians in particular for its ability to produce an impactful shot, with good *crema* (see pages 96–97) and plenty of caffeine.

You might then wonder what benefits arabica can offer? Flavour is, of course, the answer; the arabica plant produces a more nuanced product and its varieties are broad, well-defined and characterful in both their appearance and the styles of coffee that they produce. Most varieties are mutations or cross-breeds of two godfathers of arabica coffee – typica and bourbon. Typica (often simply referred to as arabica) is the variety of coffee that was first transported from Ethiopia to Yemen, then on to India. In 1718, typica samples from Java were transported to the French island of Bourbon (now known as Réunion) that lies 800 km/500 miles east of Madagascar, in the Indian Ocean. Here they mutated into a new variety, which was subsequently named bourbon. Bourbon and typica varieties now encompass the lion's share of the many varieties of arabica coffee that we see in today's coffee market.

Some of these varieties are born out of natural mutation and others are the product of the intentional cross-breeding or selection of heirloom varieties. Arabica is a self-pollinating species, so by rights the family bloodline should remain pure. But as typica and bourbon were transported to new countries and exotic climates, natural mutations took place and

The Coffee Tree.

LEFT A 19th-century colour engraving of the *Coffea arabica* species, clearly showing the fruit, flower and seeds of the plant.

ABOVE Peeling open a coffee cherry usually reveals a pair of seeds surrounded by slimy mucilage.

LEFT An arabica tree in Mexico, decorated with a full spectrum of underripe (green) and ripe (red) fruit.

many of these new variants were cultivated for their desirable features.

The story of robusta is a similar one, although the species was not officially classified until 1895 (arabica was classified in 1753). Robusta is native to Western Africa, and from there it spread throughout the world via Java. Like arabica, there are many varieties within the robusta species, but it offers little to get excited about, flavour-wise. On that note, from here on I will refer only to arabica varieties when talking generally about coffee, unless otherwise stated.

ANATOMY OF THE RAW COFFEE BEAN

Inside the coffee fruit or 'cherry' are the flat-sided kernels, which are technically seeds, but are more commonly known as beans. In each cherry, there are usually two, but sometimes – and especially on trees grown in soil containing low quantities of the micronutrient boron – there is only one, which is known as a peaberry.

'Green' or unroasted coffee beans, like most seeds, are compact stores of carbohydrates, proteins, acids and fats – basically everything the plant needs to grow and mature. Carbohydrates provide the energy that the bean would otherwise use, and makes up approximately 50 per cent of the total mass of the processed green bean. Approximately 10–20 per cent of that carbohydrate is sucrose, which will go on to provide sweetness, bittersweet caramels and even acidity later on when roasting. There's a good store of fats and proteins, too, the latter of which will react with sugar during roasting (known as Maillard reactions) to create the familiar browned appearance and corresponding flavours that we know and love.

Caffeine (a type of alkaloid) is naturally present at a level of 1–2 per cent, plus there's the lesser-known alkaloid, trigonelline, which makes up approximately 1 per cent of the bean's dry weight. Trigonelline contributes a great deal of complex bitter notes to the coffee through the chemical effect of roasting, including niacin (vitamin B3).

Finally, there's a whole host of organic acids that give us both acidity and bitterness; most important among these is chlorogenic acid (CGA), which makes up around 8 per cent of the dry mass of a green bean.

GROWING AND HARVESTING COFFEE

Virtually all of the coffee trees in the world can be found in the tropics. The typical lifespan of an arabica plant sees the plant mature from tiny seedling (or 'soldier') to flowering stage after three to five years. Shortly after it flowers, it will begin to fruit, which takes from 9–11 months to grow and ripen, and generally announces its readiness by turning a shade of vivid pinky red – although there are some varieties that produce a yellow- or orange-coloured fruit when ripe.

Coffee trees like wet, humid and shady environments, and the arabica tree in particular is sensitive to wind and high temperature. For this reason, it tends to be grown at higher altitudes; the sweet spot is usually somewhere between 1,000–2,000 m/3,300–6,600 ft elevation – any higher and the risk of frost increases.

Some arabica and robusta varieties will grow many metres high if left to their own devices, so constant pruning is required to bush out the bottom of the plant and secure the position of the fruit at an accessible height for pickers – although it's not unheard of for farm workers to use ladders.

Rather unhelpfully, coffee trees flower irregularly, resulting in ripe and unripe fruit adorning the plant at the same time. Consequentially, the mechanical harvesting of coffee in most countries is rare, and frowned upon, since it wastefully strips the tree of both ripe and unripe fruit. Couple that with the fact that many coffee farmers cannot afford to purchase such machines, as well as the difficulties presented by the invariably hilly coffee growing terrain, and it

BELOW A coffee plantation near the south-western city of Jima, Ethiopia. Until it was dissolved in 2007 this region was known as Kaffa, and thought by some to be the birthplace of coffee.

becomes very apparent that coffee farming is a highly laborious and literally 'hands-on' profession.

There are exceptions, however, and in this instance it's a very large exception. In Brazil, coffee is mostly harvested en masse, using either machines that strip both ripe, overripe and underripe fruit at the same time, or by simply shaking the tree and catching all the fruit on the ground. This slightly wasteful process is born out of a culture of quantity, not quality, farming (there are, of course, exceptions) that Brazil has become infamous for. A hundred years ago, Brazil produced over three-quarters of the coffee in the world, today it accounts for around one-third, which, at around 300,000 farms and 4 billion trees, is still an eye-watering amount.

Hand picking is not without its issues either. Some farms still insist on picking everything available and sorting it later, and even on farms that make multiple passes of the same trees, the simple instruction to pick ripe fruit is ignored as most pickers are paid by the weight of coffee they harvest. For this reason, many coffee pickers tend to grab fruit that is still a little underripe. Direct trade between roasters and farmers, where two-way communication aims to maximize the quality of the roasted product, is improving this, however, as the message that ripe fruit makes better coffee is repeatedly hammered home. In light of this, there are examples of pickers receiving rewards for harvesting ripe fruit only.

A single arabica tree can produce between 3–5 kg/6.5–11 lbs of ripe fruit in a single season, if all the elements of climate and care come together nicely. The higher end of that scale roughly equates to 1 kg/2.2 lbs of roasted beans, or 110 single espressos. Labour costs vary from country to country, but in some Central American countries, a good harvester might be capable of picking 100 kg/220 lbs of fruit in a single day, which would earn them approximately £6.50/$10, which works out as less than half a penny/half a single cent per espresso. Some coffee pickers are paid even less.

Direct trade is probably the single biggest driving force behind better-quality green beans and ensuring a fairer price for them. Take Ricardo Barbosa, for example. His farm, Fazendas Mariano, in Minas Gerais, Brazil, began supplying Origin Coffee in the UK four years ago. At the time, Ricardo consulted an agronomist to improve the running of his farm. Year

ABOVE This soldier plant will need at least another three years of maturation before it begins producing fruit.

on year, the quality and yield of the farm has improved and Fazendas Mariano now sells its coffee for almost $1 over the market level per pound.

Workforce management plays a big part in this, too, where often the picking season is relatively short and the pickers aren't full-time employees. Clever solutions to this problem are being developed, however. In Nicaragua, for example, coffee is grown on plots known as *tablones* which, due to their terroir, will cause fruit to ripen at slightly different times of the season. This allows efficient management of the pickers, who can move from one plot to another during the harvest period. In many mountainous countries, coffee is grown at altitude, where it benefits from low humidity (which lowers the risk of mould and mildew) and cooler temperatures, before it is dried and processed at lower heights that are more suitable for this part of the process. In Guatemala, for example, an altitude shift of 300 m/1,000 ft can equate to a temperature difference of as much as 5°C/41°F.

Once picked, all of the fruit goes through a machine that screens the picked cherries. Overripe (black) fruit floats, underripe (green) fruit falls through small apertures, and red (ripe) fruit is retained by the machine. Then, the green fruit is allowed to ripen off

LEFT Coffee leaf rust can be completely devastating, not just for the welfare of individual farmers, but also in terms of a country's economic output.

Such is the severity of the problem that the American Phytopathological Society recommend that coffee leaf rust should be treated as a 'continuous epidemic'. Some copper-based fungicides have proven effective in both protecting from the disease and improving fruit yield, but are largely cost-prohibitive, must be reapplied regularly, and pose a long-term danger to the condition of the soil. For many farmers, quarantine is the only available measure, which generally involves killing infected plants, along with uninfected plants within a 30 m/100 ft radius, with a mixture of diesel and herbicide.

the tree – on a patio, for example – and eventually dried and processed naturally. The red fruit is usually pulped before further processing and the already-dried cherries are sent immediately for processing. Essentially, nothing is wasted, though it's generally understood that off-the-tree ripening results in a poorer-quality coffee.

COFFEE LEAF RUST

Hemileia vastatrix, also known as 'coffee leaf rust' is a fungal parasite that targets all Coffea species. It blackens leaves, causing them to fall off and stripping the plant of most or all of its leaves. It was first reported in Kenya in 1861, and had, in just a few years, travelled to Sri Lanka (then Ceylon) and very nearly decimated the entire industry there.

Today, coffee rust is as big a problem as it has ever been. Ever-increasing temperatures and higher humidity brought on by climate change are thought to have aggravated the problem and it continues to affect not only the livelihoods of farmers, but in some cases the economic stability of entire countries. In 2013 Honduras, El Salvador and Guatemala all declared a state of national emergency during a bout of coffee leaf rust, some of them having to contend with the blighting of 70 per cent of their total crop. It looks to have hit just as hard in 2014, with Nicaragua feeling the full force of the impact.

THE COFFEE BORER BEETLE

Hypothenemus hampei, also known as the coffee weevil or *gorgojo del café* is coffee's single greatest natural predator. Native to Western Africa, the adult mites grow to 1.5 mm/$^1/_{16}$ inch in length, and unlike the rest of the insect world, are undeterred by the presence of caffeine in the coffee fruit. The beasts bore into the fruit and build tiny egg chambers – which subsequently hatch larvae – inside the coffee seed. Females fly around colonizing additional plants and males lurk about ready to perform their part in the process, never even needing to leave the fruit. If left unchecked the activities of the beetle can devastate entire harvests, with some estimates claiming the total annual global losses to be in excess of £315 million/$500 million.

Preventative measures include pesticides, but as with fungicides used against coffee leaf rust, there are associated costs and protocols that must be followed, along with environmental considerations. Traps are the most common means of dealing with the borer. Usually homemade, they may comprise a large red container (posing as a giant coffee cherry) with an ethanol solution lure inside it. An even better solution is to let another bug do the work for you... say hello to *Karnyothrips flavipes*, a type of thrip that is one of the only known natural predators of the coffee weevil. It's early days, but there's evidence to suggest that increasing the thrip population in weevil territory might be effective in keeping the parasite in check.

PROCESSING COFFEE

The way a coffee is processed before shipping sets the precedent for the style of coffee that will eventually leave the roaster. This stage of the coffee bean's life is sometimes referred to as 'wet milling' and encompasses all the various steps that occur from when the coffee is picked, right up until it is 'dry milled' and loaded into bags for transportation. Processing practices vary considerably from between regions and farms, sometimes because it is simply 'the way it's done' and other times on account of the limitations of economy or resources. In some circumstances, like in Burundi, farmers hand over their picked cherries to one of the 150 government-operated washing stations, called *sogestals*, for further processing. In other countries, on other farms, all of the processing is done by the farmer. This seemingly routine stage in the development of the coffee is far from inconsequential, however, because the effectiveness of these local interpretations open up new expressions of flavour in the coffee bean, bringing distinction to the coffee's natural profile in a way that is specific to each farm or processing facility.

Screening is usually conducted in a water tank where overripe fruit and very underripe fruit (along with leaves and sticks) will float. The ripe and underripe fruit sinks to the bottom and is then piped out ready for the next stage. However, irrespective of how meticulously the coffee has been harvested, underripe and overripe cherries are more or less inevitable. Excessively over-, or underripe fruit will, like any other fruit, result in a bad-tasting product – this is not something that a good roaster can cover up. Fruit that is perhaps only slightly underripe or overripe may meet the minimum requirements of the exporter and roaster, but cup quality will ultimately suffer, as it is the perfectly ripe fruit that contains the most sucrose, and results in the sweeter cup.

Be it the finest speciality coffee known to man, or the most deplorable coffee fruit destined for jars of instant, one way or another the coffee beans need to be removed from their fruity shell and cleaned of their slimy cherry mucilage. This is usually done in one of two ways: by wet (or washed) processing or natural (dry) processing. Some countries or regions prefer to use one method over the other, and others process using a combination of both techniques, which is known as pulped-natural or semi-washed.

NATURAL COFFEE

Naturally processed coffee is a relatively straightforward process, as all its various layers are left intact. The fruit is sent to the patio or a raised drying bed for drying and, where relevant, ripening. This process can take many weeks and care must be taken to avoid mould and rot, but some natural fermentation is normal. After the fruit has fully dried, its dark, shrivelled form must then be hulled (peeled) to reveal the beans patiently waiting inside. Brazil is the spiritual home of naturally processed coffee, where the economic culture of coffee has bred a 'pick now, sort later' approach, with the likes of São Paolo State and the Cerrado region naturally processing over 90 per cent of their coffee.

Naturally processed coffee is non-interventional, self-contained and, well, natural,

RIGHT Mechanized harvesting on one of Brazil's enormous coffee plantations.

which gives the resulting coffee its dirty, heavy and wild – often to the point of wacky – fruit notes. The capricious brilliance of dry processed coffee can yield inconsistent results, however, and the clarity of the cup can be lost. It is for this reason that some roasters choose to avoid it all together. But what it lost in finesse can be made up in body and density, which is why naturals often play important supporting roles in some of the world's best espresso blends.

WASHED COFFEE

Washed coffee, also known as wet-processed coffee, sees the whole cherry get pulped, either mechanically (by what is effectively a large

blender) or by jets of high-pressure water. Either way, the cherry is split and squeezed, forcing the beans though a separate aperture. If you really wanted to, you could pulp cherries by hand, but from personal experience I can tell you that it is slow, messy and thankless.

Pulping only deals with the soft flesh of the cherry – there's still the mucilage that coats the bean to contend with, and like the last slimy bits you get on a peach stone, it turns out it's highly resilient stuff. The tenacity of mucilage is attributed mostly to its combination of sugars and pectin, the latter of which acts both as a binding agent that is common in many fruits, and also as the gelling agent used to thicken marmalades and preserves.

Removal of the mucilage is ordinarily done by way of fermentation, which in fact refers to a broader process of microbial growth rather than the action of yeast and sugar in the absence of oxygen (as is the case with brewing). During its time spent in fermentation tanks, the pectin in the mucilage is broken down through the activity of enzymes, and the environment becomes more acidic. The length of fermentation depends on a number of factors, not least of which is temperature and the volume of coffee being processed. Experience and a good feel of the seeds will tell you when the operation has run its course. Fermentation is not just about removing mucilage, though; it's also an exercise in coffee flavour development, and, when timed well, it can produce a level of clean acidity that natural coffee can only dream of. After some washing to remove any excess mucilage, the beans are sent for drying on raised beds, or concrete floors, for around a week.

Despite the positive reputation that wet processing possesses, it is no assurance of quality. Fermentation can be unpredictable, particularly since it relies solely on micro-organisms that are naturally present on the fruit and/or in the water. Defective beans are not uncommon and most infamous of all is the 'stinker', a bean that produces a particularly unpleasant taste; this can easily damage many kilograms of roasted coffee if they

LEFT A classic hand-operated coffee pulper in Mexico works by splitting the cherries and separating the skin and flesh from the beans.

are permitted to pass along the production chain.

There are, of course, numerous variations of wet processing specific to different countries and regions, too. In Kenya, for example, it is common for two fermentations to take place, with an intermediate wash in the middle; this has been cited as one of the reasons for Kenya's incredibly bright and fruity coffees.

For farmers, the decision to dry or wet process is mostly one of economics – wet-processed coffee is widely recognized as a superior product, but it requires huge quantities of water, numerous tanks, decent plumbing and other pieces of specialist equipment. Incidentally, it's also for this reason that most robusta coffee is processed naturally, because there's little point in wasting resources on improving a fundamentally inferior product.

PULPED NATURAL COFFEE

Pulped natural coffees are recognized under a variety of other titles, including 'semi-washed', '*semi-lavado*', and the delightful-sounding 'honey-processed'. These terms don't necessarily describe identical processing methods, as with the regional differences in their names, there are differences in their methodology too – but they are all in effect a combination of natural and wet processing. For a coffee farm, this marriage of methods neatly combines the economic benefits of the natural process with some of the speed of the washed process. In the resulting cup of coffee, you tend to find better body than some washed coffees, but more clean and crisp character than with natural processing.

The process starts out in the same way as wet processing: the coffee is first pulped to remove the skin and flesh. As with washed coffee, the mucilage remains attached to the seed, but instead of being sent to fermenting tanks for removal, the beans skip straight to the drying phase. Drying pulped natural coffee is particularly challenging, as the moist and sticky environment is the perfect setting for rot and decay. Mechanical dryers don't work, as the mucilage sticks to the hot surfaces like glue, so the coffee is dried on raised beds or raked over large patios in a process that takes one to two weeks.

During pulping, the farm can also choose to remove some, or most, of the mucilage from the seed before drying, which speeds things up even more. It also gives the green bean a lighter colour, and takes the character of the coffee further in the direction of a washed coffee. Mechanical demucilagers are becoming more commonplace and are effectively an extension of the pulper, whereby they depulp and strip the mucilage through the use of rough bristles or through the use of water pressure. Critics of these types of machines claim that foregoing the fermentation process of a fully washed coffee denies the coffee some of its clarity and acidity. Interestingly, in response to this criticism, some growers are choosing to scrub and partially ferment their coffees.

LEFT This natural coffee has completed the long drying process and the dried fruit has formed a protective husk or shell.

DRYING

Whether undergoing wet processing, the pulped natural or natural method, eventually the coffee must experience a drying process that reduces the moisture content of the bean from 40 per cent down to around 10–12 per cent. This is a process that requires constant attention, since the warm, moist piles of beans need to be regularly turned to avoid the development of mould and bacteria. Airflow, temperature, humidity and light must all be taken into account.

Patios are the oldest, cheapest and simplest form of coffee drying, where the coffee is spread a couple of inches deep and raked hourly to provide equal airflow and light to all the beans. One of the useful traits of the patio is its ability to soak up the heat during the day, which it continues to release overnight, thus providing quite stable and consistent drying conditions.

Raised beds, also known as African drying beds, are becoming increasingly popular around the world. Constructed from wood and thin mesh screens, they look a lot like very long silk screens, or hammocks, that sit at waist height. The advantage of the bed is the improved airflow that it offers, meaning that the coffee does not need to be turned as regularly. Some beds, in countries such as Colombia – where the weather is changeable – also have plastic covers (like a poly-tunnel) that protect the coffee from rain, but still allow sufficient airflow. In Nicaragua and Sumatra, in Indonesia, it is common to see coffee dried on tarpaulin – a very low-cost solution.

Some hot countries, specifically those in Africa, have been forced to develop multi-stage drying processes that aim to limit the effect of the midday sun. These include such practices as moving the coffee from shade to light and piling it in mounds to moderate the evaporation of water. The general consensus is that the best coffee is produced when the rate of drying decreases near the end of the process.

As you might expect, there are also more industrial means of drying coffee, but these are not

Seeing as the amount of mucilage left on the seed is so important to the final character of the coffee – steering it in the direction of washed or natural character traits – this scrubbing or 'shaving' process is now loosely graded in the context of honey-processed coffee. 'Black honey' retains most of the mucilage before drying; 'red honey' removes some; and 'yellow honey' removes all, or nearly all of it. You can get a good idea of the extent of scrubbing simply by examining a sample of beans, where the actual colour of the beans vaguely corresponds to the style of honey processing.

Costa Rica is a good example of a country that has embraced this kind of processing with gusto. Many farmers there are investing in small demucilagers to fine-tune their processing methods. This becomes particularly interesting when a single estate releases a crop that has been processed in two or more ways, because it allows us humble consumers to draw taste comparisons between the different methods.

as commonplace as one might think. Once again it boils down to economics, where the cost of a mechanical dryer simply cannot compare with the price of cheap labour and a little bit of time. However, there is no escaping the fact that mechanical dryers at their best offer a much more consistent product, especially in areas of unpredictable weather, in a fraction of the time – usually taking just 12–24 hours from start to finish.

After drying, the coffee bean is still encased in its brittle parchment shell and will remain a relatively stable product, protected from external flavours and susceptible only to the dangers of extreme temperature and moisture. Beans are usually rested at this stage, for at least a few weeks, but only up to three months. This strengthens the cell structure of the bean and prolongs its shelf life following the dry-milling phase.

One exception to this rule can be found in Indonesia, where coffee is hulled of its parchment layer while still wet. After the coffee cherry is pulped, a brief fermentation period occurs, followed by a single wash. Then the coffee is dried for a short time and hulled of its parchment while still wet. With the premature green bean now fully exposed to the world, it is dried to the usual 10–12 per cent, *sans*-parchment, resulting in a coffee that is heavy and earthy in character – typifying the Sumatran style.

LEFTOVERS

Perhaps you're wondering what happens to all discarded coffee fruit? The coffee bean itself accounts for only around 20 per cent of the wet weight of the whole coffee cherry, so there is quite a lot of waste. In some countries, the wet pulp is recycled as fertilizer, but disposal of the vast quantities of waste water that are used in this process, and the subsequent pollution caused by coffee cherry mucilage are problems that are consistent all over the world.

Some producers have taken to drying the cherry flesh into a product called *cascara*. Resembling a dried cranberry, *cascara* can be brewed into a kind of fruit tea that tastes a little like high-octane rosehip tea, due to the caffeine present in the fruit.

BELOW Workers on this estate in Ethiopia's Yirgacheffe region dry their washed coffee on raised screens, also known as African drying beds.

MILLING AND TRANSPORTATION

To complete its journey, the coffee must be dry-milled to remove the parchment, then graded for quality, checked for defects, sampled, packed, and exported. Who, exactly, the farmer sells to in any given scenario will be based on a number of factors including – but not limited to – the size of the producer's farming operation and its financial circumstances, the degree to which the producer processes the coffee, customs in the area, geographical limitations, presence of co-operatives and the legal structure within the country.

Most growers, however, sell 'parchment' coffee (dried beans that are still encased in their endocarp, or parchment layer, while still in this form, the coffee is a mixed bag of large and small green beans, cracked beans, twigs, leaves and probably a bunch of other things besides. Since it still requires milling, screening, grading and repacking (and as much as 30 per cent of a bag

won't make the cut), parchment coffee is worth a lot less than prepared green beans. Growers sell their product either to a dry mill, which does the job of removing the parchment and sorting the coffee, an exporter (responsible for shipping the coffee) or a middleman, or even two middlemen (known colloquially as coyotes); often, these guys will hang out at bus stops and collect bags of parchment coffee from small farms, pay for them, then transport them to the mill or the exporter for sale. It's also worth noting that some dry mills export the product themselves, and some exporters operate their own dry mills.

Some growers rest, mill and sort their coffee before selling to exporters, but that is quite rare outside of the biggest farms. There are even some growers who handle their own export, too, but this is even more scarce, and not without its headaches from an importer/roaster's perspective. Some large Brazilian estates dry-mill their coffee but leave the sorting up to the exporter; this ungraded type of green coffee is called *bica corrida* there. The term translates as 'spout race', describing the practice of quickly milling and packaging the green coffee.

In some countries, there may also be a co-operative in the mix, often representing over 1,000 small growers. Co-operatives will sometimes do the job of wet milling (see page 30) and drying the coffee beans; some will also take charge of storage, before shifting the parchment coffee on to an exporter, while others may have dry-milling facilities and indeed, perform the role of the exporter.

Between every link in the supply chain, there is the possibility of a trader or broker dipping in, too. Traders can buy up stocks of coffee, add it to their inventory, then sell it on to the next man for an increased price. Brokers basically do the same thing but without ever taking physical possession of the coffee; they are in effect just connecting sellers with buyers and skimming their cut off the top. When you put it like that, it makes the role of

LEFT Even the best pickers make mistakes. This fruit will require sorting before it can be processed.

the trader and broker seem dispassionate and hard-nosed, and that can sometimes be the case, but in many scenarios it is the hard work done by these individuals that connects the best coffee with the speciality market.

In some extreme circumstances it's not uncommon for parchment coffee to pass through half-a-dozen hands before leaving its country of origin as graded green coffee, so it's not difficult to see why most farmers only receive a fraction of the coffee's final selling price. Many speciality roasters have now established direct-trade relationships with farms to better understand where their coffee has come from and to ensure the farm receives fair payment for their work. Don't be fooled by a name though; this is not a fairy-tale picture of cheerful farmers packing up containers of coffee and sending them to the door of an expectant roaster. The direct-trade relationship is more about transparency, when a farmer, miller, exporter, importer, and roaster all work together towards a more sustainable industry model. Crucially though, the roaster and farmer agree upon a fair(er) payment, and the services of the other trade partners are paid for separately.

MILLING

Once the coffee arrives at the mill, it is first passed along a vibrating platform that removes any dry

ABOVE The grading and sorting of beans is still conducted by hand and eye in many countries, including the birthplace of coffee, Ethiopia.

debris that may have been loaded into the bag. Next it is hulled of its parchment in a large blender-like contraption, and it's at this stage that the green bean itself is now finally visible. It is then sorted, and whether by hand or mechanically, the coffee will be graded according to size, density and colour. Coffee sizes are measured in fractions of an inch, but commonly referred to as a single number: eg. $^{16}/_{64}$ inch is simply a size 16. Particularly small beans may be rejected and sold at the local market.

Once sorted, samples will be taken and visually examined for defects, then roasted in a small 'sample roaster' to assess the quality of a finished cup. The mill will be looking for such things as evidence of coffee weevil activity, manifested by small boring holes in beans (see page 28).

The sheer quantity of small growers means that some exporters and buyers will sample roast, grind, brew and cup up to 1,000 samples of coffee a day. Some of these samples may be identified as being of especially high quality, and the goal of the exporter will be to separate these from the lower-quality samples that may be blended together for bulk sales. The best of these selections are made in to 'lots' destined for auction, which can vary in size from only a few pounds to many tons, depending on availability and price. Intended for the speciality market, lots may be categorized by variety, processing method, plots on the farm and even the day of harvest. Local auctions or those arranged by organizations such as 'Cup of Excellence' offer the chance for importers to connect the needs of roasters to the available product. It has become more common in the past 20 years to see roasters travel to auctions themselves to assess, cup and bid on lots in person.

When all is said and done, though, regardless of how good or bad the coffee is, someone will be willing to buy it, from chipped pieces of sorry old beans to the top tier of speciality coffee.

TRANSPORTATION

Green coffee has, in the past, always been transported In the familiar 70-kg/155-lb jute, hessian or burlap sacks and they continue to be the bag of choice for most exporters (and many a bean-bag manufacturer) as they are cheap, renewable and, practically speaking, easy to take samples from. The downside of jute is that it provides absolutely no protection from water, and as such, meets only the most fundamental requirements of a bag. Green coffee, while much hardier than roasted coffee, does age and deteriorate over time and the jute sack does little to prevent this.

In recent years, a couple of newer options have become popular with roasters that pay particular attention to the quality and freshness of their greens. One of the much-heralded alternatives is the vacuum sack, which effectively removes all of the air from around the product and protects it against moisture and exterior odours. The removal of oxygen slows the ageing of the beans until such a time that the bag is opened and the coffee roasted.

There are other plastic options that have made an appearance recently, too, such as the products created by US company GrainPro Inc., which offer some of the benefits of vacuum packing, but without the need for specialist equipment.

BELOW Germany is one of the world's biggest importers of coffee, as is evident from this new arrival at Hamburg's docks.

DECAFFEINATION

I must confess to being something of a caffeine evangelist, and those that have dared to order decaffeinated coffee from me in the past have often received it garnished with a smile of questionable sincerity. It is perhaps a little unfair of me to have acted that way, but besides those choosing to avoid caffeine before bedtime, I have never found a good reason why anyone should choose to sacrifice the quality of their coffee by choosing to drink it decaf.

Truthfully, though, decaffeinated doesn't have to mean bad. It's just a fact of life that it generally is. Most baristas apply less care and attention to making decaffeinated espresso, and certainly most roasters consider its processing and packaging an afterthought. Indeed, the green coffee destined for decaffeination is, unsurprisingly, not normally of the highest standard, a fact that is later compensated for with a dark roast.

Better-quality decaffeinated coffee is becoming more available, however, made from fresh, good-quality green beans and roasted in the correct manner, and in these rare examples we find that flavour has not been compromised at all. Confirmation of this can now be found in top cafés, where we are also starting to see dedicated decaffeinated grinders alongside a regular espresso blend.

THE PROCESS

These days, decaffeination is still conducted before the coffee is roasted and generally removes 90–95 per cent of the caffeine from the product. Priority number one is to remove as much caffeine as possible from the coffee, while priority number two is to leave behind components of the bean that are necessary for flavour development during roasting.

Today, the most sinister method of decaffeination is the solvents process, which has been used in one form or another since the early 20th century. These days, it involves either ethyl acetate (responsible for the pear-drop confectionery aroma present in nail varnish remover and glue) or dichloromethane (a type of paint stripper that is also used as a flavour extractive medium) to rinse the caffeine out of steamed green beans. It takes around 10 hours, then

ABOVE This Kafee HAG advert from 1937 promises consumers a good night's sleep after a cup of their decaffeinated coffee.

the coffee is steamed again to remove any trace of the solvents. This method of decaffeination is a very efficient process – so efficient in fact that a great deal of bean character can be stripped away, too.

The Swiss Water Process is a little more gentle, and involves first soaking the beans in water to open up their cell structure. The beans are then washed with a water-based liquid that also contains a concentrated extract of green coffee – the theory being that any positive attributes that are removed by the water are immediately replenished by the extract. The liquid is then charcoal-filtered to remove the caffeine, and subsequently recycled back around the coffee beans, sometimes multiple times.

Finally, there's the CO_2 (carbon dioxide) process, also known as Supercritical Fluid Extraction (sounds exciting, no?). Like the other methods, the coffee beans are first steamed or soaked in water to make them more porous. Following soaking or steaming, the coffee is soaked, under very high pressure, in liquid CO_2. At this stage, the CO_2 is in a supercritical state, meaning that its temperature states it should be a gas, but its pressure forces it to behave somewhere in between a gas and a liquid. The caffeine dissolves into the CO_2 over a few hours, then the pressure in the system is reduced, allowing the CO_2 to evaporate, stripping the caffeine away in the process.

On a final note, in 2008, a naturally caffeine-free species of coffee, *Coffea charrieriana*, was discovered in Cameroon, which could be a huge development.

INSTANT COFFEE

Contrary to what you might think, instant coffee is made from real coffee. Granted, it generally tastes nothing like the real thing, but once upon a time, like any other coffee drink, it was a seed on a green tree. It's the arduous inorganic process that instant coffee undergoes that strips away any hint of nuance that may or may not have once existed in what was most likely a poor and wretched coffee bean. A brewed cup of coffee is a delicate thing; its complex aromatics are fleeting, and its merits remain for only the briefest of moments. Once left to sit and wallow, a coffee loses much of its nuances, aromatics become muddy, generic and just plain clumsy.

The advantages of instant coffee are undeniable, though. Wouldn't it be wonderful to live in a world where coffee could be prepared by simply pouring hot water over coffee-flavoured granules only to be rewarded with a balanced, full-bodied and fruity cup? The coffee would always be consistent, foolproof to prepare, easy to adjust

according to strength preferences and it would never go stale – not to mention the fact that it would take up much less space in the kitchen.

That, no doubt, was the plan when David Strang launched Strang's Coffee, the first soluble coffee granule back in 1890. Strang used a 'Dry Hot-Air' method to evaporate the moisture out of brewed coffee, leaving behind a crusty coffee residue that could be broken up into mostly soluble nuggets. Who knows what it tasted like – there's a good chance it was terrible – but the idea was ingenious and it prompted other companies to seek new, convenient ways to brew coffee in the home.

One such product was George Constant Washington's 'Red E Coffee' (see what he did there?), which launched in 1910 and dominated the market until the arrival of Nescafé. Perhaps the biggest name in instant coffee, Nescafé, was launched in 1938 after the Brazilian government approached the Nestlé food company, seeking a solution for its huge surplus of coffee beans. The product itself was a combination of sugar and dried coffee residue, and was an immediate success, thanks largely to World War II, as it became a hit with the military for its longevity and convenience. After the war, it became a staple product in kitchen cupboards around the world. At the height of its popularity in the 1970s, over one-third of all the coffee imported into the USA was being turned into instant.

After World War II, high-vacuum freeze-drying was introduced, which meant that the coffee could be dried at a lower temperature, more quickly, meaning the flavour was better preserved. This technology, along with spray drying, is how instant coffee is made today.

In all methods the coffee is first roasted and ground. Next water is pumped through a series of 5–7 huge percolation columns. Each column contains coffee at varying stages of extraction, and as the water passes from the freshest through to the oldest, the temperature decreases, ensuring that nothing is left behind. Basically it's the most efficient (and impassive) method of extracting flavour from ground coffee that modern industry has allowed us. So far, so apathetic. Next the extract is concentrated to around 40 per cent solids. This can be done in a couple of ways, the easiest and most damaging of which is simple heating and evaporation. Another option is to put the coffee in a massive centrifuge which, like a spin dryer, will separate the heavy (flavoursome) components from the light (watery) bits. The final option is the technique of partially freezing the solution, causing ice (water) crystals to form, which can be mechanically separated from the gooey coffee mush. While these heinous acts are committed, the airspace around the coffee is flushed with nitrogen and/or carbon dioxide, which preserves some of the aroma of the coffee by eliminating oxygen from the system. Next the concentrate is either spray-dried, or freeze-dried.

Spray-drying entails moving a superfine mist of coffee concentrate through a column of hot air – think hairspray and hair dryer. The mist is so fine that the tiny coffee particles dry into big piles of brown flour. The 'flour' is then tumbled through the air with a fine mist of steam, which wets the surface of the dry coffee causing the dust particles to adhere together and form the little nuggets that we are familiar with.

Freeze-drying is slightly more sympathetic to the coffee. The concentrate is cooled down to -40°C/-40°F usually very rapidly (in the region of 1–2 minutes). The very low temperature means that the coffee concentrate is below its triple point – the lowest temperature possible for solid and liquid concentrate phases to co-exist. This is important because the next stage aims to remove the frozen water from the concentrate by sublimation: i.e. turning it into vapour, rather than melting. This is achieved by dramatically lowering the air pressure inside the freeze-dryer and simultaneously increasing the temperature. It is done over different stages, but the aim is simple: get rid of the water and leave behind only moon-rock-esque coffee.

The dried coffee will still contain around one per cent moisture, but compared to most earthly objects that is very low indeed, and the cause for its fragile and brittle nature. It's this low water content that also gives instant coffee one of its greatest strengths: preservation. But it also means it must be stored in a sealed container to prevent it from sucking water out of the air like a sponge.

It's not clear whether it is the technology used to manufacture instant coffee, or the quality of the coffee in the first place, which is responsible for the insipid instants that we know and recognize. My own experiences with freeze-dryers leads me to think that there is perhaps a future for genuinely great instant coffee.

Right now, though, the speciality coffee movement and the supermarket shelf are at odds with each other. The instant coffee consumer will see little value in an instant costing five times the price of the industry standard, and the gourmets themselves will not lower to the romantically vacuous realms of instant – even if it did taste any good.

BELOW Convenience, evocative marketing and blind ignorance to the quality of flavour helped to build a market for soluble coffee.

It was all perfect from the starter to the coffee. Now you can relax.

The after dinner coffee is the one part of the meal you don't have to worry about – as long as you're serving Gold Blend.

Gold Blend Instant Coffee is made only from selected beans, which are roasted, brewed, and freeze-dried to lock in that very special flavour until you release it.

Which means you get a coffee so good, you can serve it at whatever strength your guests prefer to drink it, and they'll still enjoy the full rich taste of fresh-ground coffee.

For that full rich taste of fresh ground coffee – serve Gold Blend.

COFFEE AS A COMMODITY

Since the 1940s, there have been ongoing arrangements between producing countries (many of which rely on coffee as the chief export) and consuming countries that have aimed to stabilize production quotas to limit overproduction and the economy-shattering price drops they can cause. The Inter-American Coffee Agreement, first signed in 1940 and the International Coffee Agreement (ICA) of 1962, like so much of coffee's history, have their roots in politics, born out of the concern that Latin-American countries may be tempted into extreme left or right wing political tendencies if their export values weren't guaranteed. Today, the ICA is managed by the International Coffee Organization (ICO) and now includes members from 42 producing countries, equating to about 97 per cent of all the coffee grown in the world, according to the ICO website. The agreement is only really relevant to the commodities market, where coffee is purchased at the lowest-possible price, destined for a jar of instant or a pack of some stepped-on, pre-ground, black crumbs. In effect, the agreement means that each producing country has a production quota, and when the price per pound falls, the quota is reduced and the price, in theory, goes up.

Of course the commodity price for a pound of coffee still fluctuates, so there is a kind of baseline price that everyone works from, often referred to as the 'C-price', that acts as global indicator of the price of commodity coffee. The C-price actually only refers to the price of coffee on the New York Stock Exchange (NYSE), so it isn't indicative of the price being paid everywhere (since only a small percentage of coffee passes through NYSE), but it does act as a reference point for other markets. Subject to the countless variables that can affect any high-volume product, the 'C' is prone to shift considerably, and in the past five years alone, it has dropped to barely more than $1/65 pence per pound in late 2013, and peaked at a massive $3/£1.90 per pound in 2011. Since the C-price is not reflective of the cost of production of a pound of coffee, this has meant that sometimes producers find themselves losing money.

FAIR TRADE, ORGANIC AND RAINFOREST ALLIANCE

Up until the later part of the 20th century, the stark reality of poverty, exploitation, violence and political corruption that the coffee industry has aggravated, in many countries over the years had been quite well covered up. The ICA, which was renegotiated every five years, expired in 1989 after failing to agree on new export quotas, and parties failed to establish new terms quickly enough. What ensued was a 'coffee crisis' that saw the supply of coffee vastly outweigh the demand. This drove down the price of coffee to only $0.77/50 pence per pound as the market became saturated, which spelled bad news for millions of farmers across the world. The Fair Trade Certification, under its original name, 'Max Havelaar'– the hero of a 19th-century Dutch novel that critiques the practices of the Dutch East India Company in Java – was

LEFT Coffee is the chief export of over a dozen developing countries; in Uganda it makes up 15 per cent of the country's total output.

launched in the Netherlands, and aimed to standardize pricing, no matter what the availability of coffee at the time. Now known by the more familiar name 'Fair Trade', the price per pound of green coffee is set at $1.40/90 pence, or $0.05 (0.03 pence) above the C-price (whichever is greater).

On the whole, Fair Trade has to be a good thing if, as it claims, it is giving more money to coffee producers. The critics of Fair Trade will argue that there is insufficient transparency in the process, traceability is poor (only co-operatives can enrol in the program) and that the simple freezing or tracking of prices does little to encourage farmers to improve the quality of their coffee.

The other two official certifications of note are Organic and Rainforest Alliance. The former, as with any other product or foodstuff, simply indicates that the farming practices that have been used to produce the product are in-line with organic standards, promoting good soil health and sustainability of farmland. An organic certification has no bearing on quality, though. A Rainforest Alliance certification is often (but not always) partnered with an organic certification, as it goes a step further, requiring certain agricultural practices that promote sustainability, safeguarding of the environment, as well as welfare standards for producing families and their communities.

SPECIALITY COFFEE

Speciality Coffee is a term that has been used since the mid-1970s to describe coffee of high quality and value that is in some way representative of its origin, variety or growing and processing practices. The

ABOVE Direct trade relationships between farm and roaster pursue better transparency and a fairer price for coffee.

ABOVE LEFT Certifications like those pictured guarantee some farming and trade standards, but have no bearing on coffee quality.

speciality coffee model sees roasters negotiate the price of a coffee with a broker, importer, leadership representatives from a co-operative, or in some cases, the owner of a mill or a farm itself. Coffee is also sometimes sold at auction in the country of its origin, where roasters and importers bid for specific 'lots'. The price paid for speciality coffee varies according to the C-price and its country of origin, but also, of course, according to its quality.

Some roasters have, in recent years, begun building relationships with growers and in some cases dealing directly with them, known as a 'Direct Trade' relationship (see pages 34–35). The obvious benefits are that the farmer gets a fair price, the roaster has improved traceability of his product, and in some cases the ability to work with the farm on improving future seasons' crops.

'Relationship Coffee' is another term that is sometimes used by speciality roasters. As with Direct Trade, the definition is slightly vague; neither of them are certifiable guarantees, and as such are subject to the possibility of being abused and misused. Relationship Coffee usually means that there is an ongoing dialogue between the roaster and the grower in an effort to improve coffee quality and traceability.

ROASTING COFFEE

03

THE ROLE OF THE ROASTER

We all know that roasting the coffee beans is an essential stage on the road to a mug of coffee. But its necessity aside, this keenly observed and succinct process that gracefully traverses the line between science and art, is nothing short of meteoric in its lasting effect on the character of the coffee. Decisions made at the roasting stage (as with most things in coffee) are irreversible, and it is for the home brewer, perhaps the most important stage of the entire chain of events that takes us from farm to cup. I know that's a bold statement, and, practically speaking many of the cups of coffee you are served on the high street likely fall foul through no major fault of the roaster, but it would not be outrageous to suggest that the skill of the person who roasted the coffee that you are drinking right now has the larger part to play in the quality of the cup.

And this, in a sense, is the quandary of the roaster. To better illustrate this, let's compare coffee to wine for a moment. In wine production, the winemaker manages most, if not all, of the quality-control points of the product, from growing, harvesting, juicing and fermenting through to filtering and bottling. The quality of the way it is served, however, is secured only by the consumer pouring the liquid at the appropriate temperature and finishing it within a sensible period of time. In coffee, on the other hand, the baton is carried on a frail and tenuous journey, each step accumulating the collective skill of all its previous keepers. The work of the first person and every person afterwards is all for nothing if the baton is dropped on the last leg, just as the tireless endeavours of a farmer in Nicaragua are wasted on a clueless barista.

Any of the key people in the formation could claim that their reputation is in the hands of the other key players as, in normal circumstances, their powers only stretch as far as who they buy their product from, what they do with it once they have it, and who they sell it to. But it is the roaster who plays the most obvious middleman role between the beginning and end, and it's the roaster that we, the consumer, best associate with. Folk will happily stroll into a random café safe in the knowledge that their favourite roaster supplies the coffee; while it may be naive to assume that the expertly roasted coffee from 'Roaster X' will be prepared consistently by the hundreds of cafés that it supplies, not to mention the thousands of staff that the those cafes employ, it has become clear in recent years that the after-sales support and training that the roaster provides (along with the culling of those cafés that fail to uphold the necessary standard) is just as important as the product that gets loaded into its bags.

THE SKILL OF THE ROASTER

Roasters will buy coffee based on a number of factors; flavour is, of course, one of the most important, and this will in part be a reflection of how

LEFT This bag of Nicaraguan coffee clearly indicates the year of harvest, variety, farm and processing method ('lavado' translating as 'washed').

and when the coffee was picked, processed, graded, packaged and imported, and how these factors balance with price. Sustainability and ethics also play a part these days, so questions arise about how much a farm is being paid per pound of coffee, how sustainable the agricultural methods of the farm or estate is, and how the growers are being paid, if the coffee is the product of a co-operative effort from numerous smaller growers.

Once the coffee is in hand, then it's the skill of the roaster that shapes the final character of the coffee and connects the dots between origin, terroir and specific variety with those of brewing method and cup quality. But it's important to remember that bad green coffee can be tamed, but not entirely saved, by the hands of a great roaster, just as a bad roaster – or an average roaster for that matter – can very easily corrupt even the finest speciality beans.

Mastering the roast is an art form that can be likened to few others. The complex chemistry and physics of roasting coffee have been the subject of hundreds of books and research papers, as scientists attempt to identify the flavourful and aromatic constituents of good roasted coffee, and work out where they came from. Naturally, an understanding of the workings of the roaster itself is important, but an understanding of the green coffee and a clear vision of positive attributes that it harbours are also key.

ABOVE Piles of coffee beans at various degrees of roasting, from green (unroasted) at the bottom left to dark brown (French roast) at the top left.

Those with their hands on the gas knob have adopted practices, tweaked their methods and tasted a lot of coffee in search of a better product. Today, our understanding of roasted coffee is better than it has ever been, but the growing realization that coffee is enormously complex has only really cemented a feeling of acceptance as to how powerless we are to truly affect and select its attributes on a molecular scale. Sure, through some trial and error and perhaps some referencing of past roasts, we might be able to highlight a peach-like acidity in Ethiopian Yirgacheffe coffee, or a chocolate character from Brazilian Daterra coffee, but hand-picking attributes with any level of precision is no easier than opening your fridge door and expecting a roast dinner to fall out.

Part of coffee's beauty is its ambiguity; it's not roasted to an exact recipe of aldehydes, acids, sugars, carbonyls, caramels, carotenoids and other aromatic molecules in a perfect digital formula of saturation, contrast and brightness. Roasters are more like impressionist painters, where the artistry may be vague, imbalanced and imprecise, but the resulting composition as a whole can depict a richer, more emotional story through its imperfections.

THE EVOLUTION OF THE COFFEE ROASTER

The modern coffee roaster represents over 500 years of acquired knowledge. Improvements in design only became necessary once it had been established what was wrong with the equipment available at the time. A better design meant a better product, which would command a higher price for both the machine and the coffee it produced. Bigger designs were only needed once casual home roasters accepted that commercially roasted coffee was of a higher standard and more consistent than the stuff they were making on their fireplaces.

Looking through the evolution of the roaster, there are three fundamental issues that the inventors have fought with. First is the even distribution of heat through the coffee bean mass, which we know gives a consistent and better-quality roast. Second is the speeding up of the process of loading and unloading the roaster, which increases throughput (the rate of production or the rate at which something can be processed) and decreases labour cost. Third is the ability to monitor the roast by way of visual, or physical access to the coffee beans, which results in clearer precision and ultimately a better product.

EARLY ROASTING

We will probably never know exactly when the first coffee roasters came into existence, since they almost certainly evolved organically from the regular cooking equipment of the day. Stone bowls and clay cups were certainly popular options, left to sit over hot coals or an open fire, and occasionally stirred to ensure even bean browning. They got the job done, of course, but scorched bean surfaces and underdeveloped centres were commonplace.

The first known dedicated coffee roaster made an appearance in Persia in the early 1400s. This roasting plate was like a large perforated spoon, designed to sit above an open fire pit or brazier and roast small quantities of coffee at a time; the holes in the plate tell us that early coffee drinkers recognized the importance of convection and good airflow in the roasting process. Similar designs

BELOW RIGHT This Italian street scene from the early 20th century bears a striking similarity to the adjacent image.

BELOW A 1774 engraving from Vienna shows coffee being roasted on an open brazier in the street.

followed, increasing in size and coming to resemble a large metal spider crouching over hot coals.

The concave nature of the early roasting spoons also points to a general understanding of the importance of movement during roasting, to better aid even cooking. Further enhancements were made through the 16th century, culminating in Ottoman-inspired long-handled frying pans, with sealed lids, and a long paddle – not dissimilar to a copper bedpan – that could be turned to agitate the beans.

Cylindrical coffee roasters were the first major breakthrough. They came about in the mid-17th century and were probably of Turkish origin. Mounted over an open fire and generally constructed from tin plate or tin-coated copper, these roasters were sealed units, turned by hand, in efforts to keep the beans moving and, they believed, keep the aroma well contained. Whether recognized at the time, or not, these cylinders would have been a great improvement over the 'open pan' approach, through the uninterrupted shifting of the beans as well as the protection from open flames that they offered. By 1660, these cylindrical roasters were popping up in London, one example being Elford's white iron machine, which was 'turned on a spit by a jack' and considered a huge technological leap forward, since the use of human labour (usually in the form of a small boy) was no longer required.

It was perhaps the Dutch who took the most serious approach to coffee roasting equipment, as attested by Humphrey Broadbent, 'the London coffee man' in 1722:

'I hold it best to roast coffee berries in an iron vessel full of little holes, made to turn on a spit over a charcoal fire, keeping them continually turning, and sometimes shaking them that they do not burn, and when they are taken out of the vessel, spread 'em on some tin or iron plate 'till the vehemency of the heat is vanished; I would recommend to every family to roast their own coffee, for then they will be almost secure from having any damaged berries, or any art to increase the weight, which is very injurious to the drinkers of coffee. Most persons of distinction in Holland roast their own berries.'

The Dutch-born 'iron vessel' that Broadbent refers to was the first wide-scale roasting solution for the household fireplace. Like Elford's invention, it consisted of a closed cylindrical chamber of around 20 cm/8 inches in length, but featured a sliding door for the beans to be dropped through. The end of the roaster would be hung on the hook of the traditional fireplace crane and the wooden handle turned slowly to facilitate the roasting of the beans.

This type of roaster subsequently evolved to become a free-standing contraption of larger proportions, also sporting a metal hood to help heat retention, more commonly used by coffee shops.

THE EMERGENCE OF COMMERCIAL ROASTING

Much of the coffee roasting that was taking place in Europe at the time was in the family home, in part because it wasn't considered a skilled practice, and partly because it was an assurance of authenticity. Also, up until the end of the 18th century, roasters had pretty much all been small-scale pieces of kit, capable of processing no more than a few kilos of beans at a time. Home roasting was a slow means to an end, though, sometimes taking up to an hour, which yielded coffee that had a baked character, lacking in acidity and bite.

But this was the era of innovation across all industries, from dairy farming and distilling to textiles and paper-making, with new technology successfully cutting back the required workforce and improving quality and throughput. Coffee roasting was no exception.

The tentative first steps came in 1824, when Richard Evans patented the first large-scale commercial coffee roaster. Besides its size, the cylindrical roaster had a few added benefits over anything that had come before, including the facility to easily up-end the entire roaster to remove the beans from the roasting chamber. Evans' design also designated a tube and 'examiner' that could be used to take samples from the roaster during roasting – a crucial step forward in the pursuit of quality.

In the mid-19th century, quick unloading and re-loading was an ongoing challenge that many inventors sought to provide a solution for, along with design modifications intended to help the roaster determine when the coffee was ready. One of the most innovative, yet slightly over-engineered solutions has to be Daussé's scale roaster. Dating back to 1846, this French- designed piece worked on the principle that coffee loses around 15–20 per cent of its weight

THE EMERGENCE OF THE MODERN DRUM ROASTER

The undisputed father of the modern commercial coffee roaster is surely the London-born, but subsequently New-York-based, Jabez Burns. The Burns roasters of the 1860s and 1870s sported two major improvements over previous designs, both of which can be identified in contemporary drum roasters. The first was a series of flanges placed on the inside of the roasting drum – essentially a modified Archimedes-screw design – once confusingly described by Burns as 'a double right and left augur, one within the other, firmly secured together and also to the shell or cylinder'. The screw continuously directed the flow of coffee beans back and forward through the length of the drum, achieving even heat distribution throughout the bean mass and scoring bonus points for easy unloading of the roasted coffee without the need to remove the drum.

Burns' second innovation was in the field of post-roast cooling, in which he was one of the pioneers. In an 1867 design, he pioneered a method of drawing cool air through a bed of roasted coffee, speeding up the cooling-down process, and no-doubt improving the quality of the product. Modern drum roasters have cooling trays that work under the same principles.

There were explorations into different fuels during this time, too. Early industrial roasters were heated with coal, coke or peat, which in many instances would have almost certainly contributed a smoky taste to the coffee, and in the case of coal, possibly imparted carcinogens into the coffee. Natural gas was a welcome arrival when it began hitting European and American cities in the mid-19th century, since it was both smokeless and far easier to control. Most commercial roaster manufacturers switched over to manufacturing gas models from the 1880s onwards, but there were still coal-powered models being released well into the 20th century.

Spherical roasters, like large iron globes, which aimed to better distribute heat, had a brief spell of popularity at the turn of the century, but these designs soon lost favour over the easier-to-operate

(mostly through water loss) during roasting. Beans were weighed before loading, then a target weight, relative to the desired degree of roast and the country of origin of the beans, was calculated. The roaster itself was suspended from a scale, balanced by a set of target weights on the reverse side, which caused the roaster to lift up during roasting once the calculated weight loss was achieved. It worked alright, but still required an arm to turn the drum.

But as consumers placed greater faith in the convenience of 'pre-roasted' coffee, bigger roasters were needed, and who better to supersize a roaster than America? James W. Carter of Boston patented the design for his pull-out roaster in 1846, a system that became the commercial roaster of choice for the following two decades. The Carter roaster was basically a manually turned sheet-iron drum, about the size of a large wine barrel, that was fixed into a brick coal furnace. It had one major difference, though: loading and unloading of the coffee was performed by ejecting the whole drum from the furnace and opening a door on the side. Before doing this, a bucket of water would be tossed into the roaster to kick-start the cooling, then the roasted coffee was ejected and promptly raked across the floor, filling the room with steam. In this way, the furnace itself maintained its heat and batches could be run through faster.

Entire banks (or batteries) of Carter roasters were installed in the largest coffee roasting companies of the time – such as the Dwinell-Wright Company of Boston.

drum. By the early part of the 20th century, the template for the modern roaster had been more or less set in stone, exemplified by the likes of Probat's 'Perfekt' roaster, released in 1907, with its electrically powered drum on a horizontal axis, a gas heat source and a cyclone set-up to assist in cooling the roasted beans and removing chaff.

Further advances, far-reaching in their effect but comparatively small in their alteration to the basic design, have been welcomed by roasteries through the 20th century. The development of the double drum and indirect firing are perhaps the two most significant in terms of improving coffee quality. Both of these technologies have increased the speed, consistency and precision of roasting, the first by reducing scorching of the bean surface and the second by reducing the temperature of the roast while at the same time increasing the rate at which heat is applied. Control systems on modern roasters have reached a state of sophistication today that not only allows complete control over temperature, airflow, recirculation of air, drum rotation, cooling

ABOVE Female volunteers roasting coffee at Cadby Hall for Joseph Lyons and Co. in London's Hammersmith during World War I.

mechanisms and after-burn, but also the computerized profiling of such things, completely tailored to the requirements of the bean.

Today, it's German-made roasters that continue to lead the way in drum roasting, with Probat, which took over Jabez Burns in 1998 in assuming the role of the most highly revered name in coffee-roasting circles – a hard-earned status that awards the company a large chunk of the speciality coffee pie. Two Turkish roasters, Toper and Garanti (both founded in the 1950s), continue to produce good-quality machines, as well as Dutch roaster manufacturer Giesen. Exciting things are coming out of America, too, from the well-respected names of Diedrich and Loring, the former of which manufactures beautiful traditional-style drums, and the latter, which has become well known for its 'Smart Roast' automated system.

HOW ROASTERS WORK

Modern coffee roasters can take anywhere from 7–20 minutes to get the job done and can be conducted in a whole manner of ways, from a humble 250 g/9 oz. counter-top roaster to a computerized million-dollar behemoth. The goal is the same: develop flavour and aroma through the application of heat.

Pulling apart the process a little more, roasting is broadly a three-stage procedure, with the first two stages overlapping somewhat. First, the beans are loaded into the roaster, where the coffee beans dry, as water migrates from inside the bean to the surface. This stage is not particularly impactful from a visual standpoint, but it is detectable through a grassy, warm-hay aroma that the steam gives off. This leads on to stage two, the proper roasting, where complex caramelization and browning reactions that give us the familiar coffee flavour. The coffee bean becomes less dense, drier, and more brittle during roasting – factors that combine to make it more porous and its components more soluble. Finally, when the roast is deemed to be complete, the beans are dropped out and stage three, cooling and outgassing, ensues.

TYPES OF HEAT TRANSFER

Almost all coffee roasters cook beans through a combination of different types of heat transfer: conduction, convection and radiation.

Heating by conduction is very simple to understand. It is the transfer of energy that takes place when a hot, solid object makes contact with a cooler solid object: for example, when you pick up a cup of hot coffee and your hand warms up. The same thing happens during the roasting of coffee beans when cool beans touch the hot surface of the roaster, and also when a slightly hotter bean touches a slightly cooler bean.

Conduction shouldn't be mistaken for radiant heat, however, which is where the hot surface of

LEFT This modern drum roaster is controlled by computer software, capable of producing highly consistent results.

the roaster, or even a coffee bean, emits infrared radiation and heats things nearby, but not through direct contact with it – the radiator in a house works like this.

Convection occurs where a liquid or gaseous heat source – in the case of a coffee roaster this is the air – moves as a continuous current, rapidly transferring energy as it goes. A convection (or fan) oven works in this way, which is why it cooks faster even at lower temperatures than a traditional gas oven.

Heat transfer by convection is the preferred method of cooking for coffee roasters, because it requires lower temperatures and less energy, yet rather conveniently, convection is also quicker. But when all is said and done, coffee beans cook mostly by conduction, since once convective heat rapidly permeates the outer layer of the coffee, it can then only transfer through the static structure of the bean through conduction from one solid layer to another. Convection speeds up this process.

THE DRUM ROASTER

The drum roaster is still the roaster of choice for a great deal of the global coffee industry, and in particular it remains the darling of the speciality coffee industry, now taking pride of place in many of the world's best cafés. Its timeless tumble-dryer design, range of available sizes, and simple, yet highly customizable roasting process, have firmly secured its position in some of the world best roasteries.

Classic examples of drum roasters comprise a rotating drum made of solid steel or iron, usually encased within a slightly larger drum and mounted on a horizontal axis. Single-drum varieties also exist, but the convection and radiation of heat between the two skins of a double-drum roaster are thought to result in a more even cook. Traditionally, the cylinder is heated from below by a gas flame, and somewhere above the drum is an exhaust that draws up smoke, steam and any other roast by-products. Beans are loaded in by way of a hopper (the part of the machine that stores the beans before they are loaded) on top of the drum and, once finished, are ejected out of the front of the machine into a wide cooling tray. A fan draws air downwards, through the roasted beans, while rotating bristled arms stir them around.

Indirectly heated drum roasters pump hot air into the roasting drum from an external heat source. This means the drum temperature is much cooler than if it were directly heated and, crucially, the air temperature of the roaster can be that little bit higher to compensate. The natural progression from this is the economically sound 'recirculating drum roaster,' which recycles some of the hot exhaust air back into the roasting chamber. This kind of roaster is thought to provide a more stable roasting environment, thanks to higher humidity in the airflow, which in turn curtails the menace of bean surface burning.

FLUID-BED ROASTERS

Fluid-bed roasters are a relatively new invention, first trialled by the late Michael Sivetz of Corvallis, in Oregon, who passed away in March 2012. Sivetz patented the first fluid bed roaster in 1976, with the motto 'keep beans moving', which it has to be said, is exactly what these contraptions do.

Because fluid-bed roasters work on the principle of balancing bean mass, temperature and airflow, they are even more sensitive to roast-batch size than classic drum roasters. If the load is too small, the beans tend to bounce around in chaotic waves, interfering with currents and leading to an uneven roast. If the load is too large, the upward air pressure from the blower is insufficient to propel the beans into a fluid motion, and the lower layers cook like the base of a pizza.

Since these machines come in both manual and automatic flavours, the airflow on manual models needs to be dialled down through the course of the roast as the coffee beans become lighter. The upside of this kind of roasting is that almost all of the heat transfer to the surface of the bean is by convection in the fast-moving air currents, which makes the process faster. Much faster in fact, with some light roasts lasting only 3–4 minutes.

Fluid-bed roasters also have little or no moving parts, which reduces the risk of malfunction. The downside is that fluid-bed roasters capable of even 5-kg/11-lb batch sizes are scarce, and even then require huge amounts of energy to keep the beans moving around.

OTHER TYPES OF ROASTER

Centrifugal coffee roasters are generally only seen in large scale applications, where their gigantic capacity and quick roasting time mean that some models can churn out up to 4,000 kg/8,800 lbs an hour! As the name suggests, they comprise a huge dish that spins on a vertical axis, a bit like the tea-cup fairground ride. Heat is typically fired down in the centre of the dish as the spinning action flings the mass of the coffee towards the curved outside edge. This centrifugal force shoots the beans up the side of the machine, then numerous small fins split them into uniform streams that direct the flow back into the centre of the roaster to repeat the process. The effect is like that of a doughnut-shaped maelstrom of rolling coffee beans, and both the speed they move, along with the rate of airflow, mean that a roast can be complete in only 5–6 minutes.

Not content with loading and unloading your roaster with 500 kg/1,100 lbs at a time? Well, if money is no object, perhaps a continuous coffee roaster is for you. Like the steam-punk-inspired elongated drum roaster, these monsters can accept a non-stop flow of green coffee beans, which travel along the length of the drum like a journey into the fiery pits of hell, roasting as they go. As you might expect, the roast profile is controlled by a computer, which adjusts airflow, air temperature and the drum speed to tailor the end product.

Tangential roasters are, upon first glance of their inner workings, quite similar to drum roasters. However, these massive enclosed boxes are a little more clever when it comes to airflow than your traditional drum. Beans are rotated on a horizontal axis and hot air is channelled downward (at a tangent to the drum) allowing it to whip through the bean mass and exit out of the top of the roaster. The advantage of this kind of roasting is the clean fluidity of hot air currents, which improves the rate of heat conduction from the

bean's surface to the bean's interior. Technology like this is advantageous to everyone, but especially those roasters buying lower-grade beans of a non-uniform size and density – which of course tends to be those with a need for a higher rate of production.

Many of these large-scale roasters have fought to overcome the issue of cooling half a ton of hot, roasted coffee. Some have 'quenching' systems, where a fine mist of water is sprayed onto the bean immediately after roasting; this doesn't actually 'wet' the bean as such, but causes it to cool as the water draws latent heat from the bean. Studies suggest that it speeds up the outgassing, too. Quenching systems are usually coupled with more

ABOVE A drum roaster's cooling tray, where hundreds of litres of cool air are drawn through the mass of hot beans. Stopping the cooking process quickly is an essential component of a good roast.

traditional (and sometimes not so traditional) air cooling. Cutting-edge designs feature powerful air turbines that blast air at a sufficient speed to levitate hundreds of kilograms of roasted beans in an incessant storm of super-cooled air.

For the remainder of this chapter, all references to roasters in general, unless otherwise specified, will relate to the drum roaster, since it is by far and away the most popular design used in speciality coffee today.

WHAT HAPPENS WHEN COFFEE IS ROASTED

Green beans don't taste of much and they're tricky to grind down into a powder. If you get a good enough blender (don't risk breaking your coffee grinder) and brew them into a tea (since it really cannot be called coffee, and you'll find something thin, faintly acidic, grassy and insipid. There, I've spared you the bother.

It is roasting that unlocks all of the hidden treasures that the green bean guards within its highly organized and densely packed stores of fats, acids and sugars. The coffee oils that will be later converted into flavoursome molecules are at this time tightly packed against the cell walls of the plant, and it is only through roasting that the true soluble character of the coffee bean can be discovered. But 'true' is perhaps the wrong word, as there is no set-in-stone destination for a coffee bean on the journey to roasted glory.

The roaster's primary goal is to cook the coffee to the required level of doneness, tailored to the specific coffee and its intended use once roasted. Lighter roasts tend to exhibit more of the coffee's natural character (good or bad) and lend themselves well to more traditional brewing methods. Darker roasts will replace much of the coffee's natural character traits with the brown roast character that we are all so familiar with – and it's for this reason that poor-quality coffee is almost exclusively dark-roasted. Darker roasts find themselves at home in espresso, however, where the nature of the brewer dictates that lighter coffees become overwhelmingly acidic.

The secondary goal of the roaster, which, in truth, is every bit as important as the primary goal, is that of carefully controlled coffee bean development. In a highly generalized sense, if the roast takes too long and/or is too cool, the coffee will exhibit a weaker, slightly 'baked' character when brewed; if roasted too quickly and/or too hot, then there's a risk that the interior of the bean will be underdeveloped and the resulting coffee will tend towards spiky, sour, bitter or smoky characteristics.

There is no tertiary goal, only the pursuit of deliciousness. We will cover some more roasting techniques in detail later, but let's first take an in-depth look at what happens to the coffee bean during a typical roast.

THE ROASTING PROCESS

All drum roasters have an optimum batch size of beans that they can handle. Overload the roaster and you may find that proceedings slow down with detrimental effect; load too few beans in and you risk surface burns on the beans as they slide around, deprived of the tumbling action that larger numbers grant them. The roaster will aim to heat the coffee as quickly as possible in the early stages of the roast, and it is for this reason that the roaster is always pre-heated before the beans are dropped in.

As roasting rapidly warms the bean, moisture begins to migrate towards the surface of the bean and evaporate away. The rate at which this happens is dependent on temperature, bean mass, bean density and airflow, but under normal roaster conditions the water content of the bean will typically drop from 11 per cent to 2 per cent in around 5–7 minutes. At the earlier stages of the roast, the bean sometimes becomes slightly paler, or more milky-looking, before turning a more orange and eventually cinnamon colour in the later

LEFT A handful of green coffee beans: pretty, patient and, alas, largely flavourless.

stages. This early sector is known commonly as the 'drying' phase.

There's more to this stage than just drying, however, as important steps are also occurring in the development of sweetness, acidity and bitterness (arising from the breakdown of chlorogenic acids and sugar), which will make themselves known in the flavour of the resulting cup. This part of the roast also sees the start of another set of chemical changes: Maillard reactions.

Maillard reactions are browning effects caused by interactions between amino acids and sugars. They occur at all temperatures, but much more rapidly when heat is applied, and especially above 150°C/300°F. These reactions are brain-achingly complex in their nature, but the most important thing to understand is that they are largely responsible for the flavours that we associate with such delectable foodstuffs as browned meat, baked bread and toasted cereals. They are also the reason for the brown colour in roasted coffee.

By this stage, there will be no shortage of aroma emanating from the roaster. The sentiment that the smell of roasting coffee (and even 'freshly roasted coffee' for that matter) is to some a sacrosanct intoxicant, triggering olfactory pleasure to the point of physical debilitation, was clearly circulated by someone who had never visited a coffee roastery. During the drying phase, roasting coffee smells like stale popcorn, wet hay and cold toast. Later on, it simply smells like oven-baking a bunch of sticks. To the experienced roaster, it is alleged that aroma can proffer some indication of doneness, but these are not the stirring scents of aromatic transcendence that one might imagine.

As the bean dries, it also expands, and a fine membrane layer, which is difficult to see on a green bean, emerges and begins to peel away. This is known as the silverskin while it remains part of the bean, and once it becomes detached, it is demoted to the rather more humble-sounding chaff. Chaff is harmless in terms of its ability to affect coffee quality, but it is a concern when it comes to the removal and collection from the roaster, due to its potential as a fire risk should sufficient quantities of it be left to build up.

As the drying phase comes to a close, the increase in bean temperature further forces the

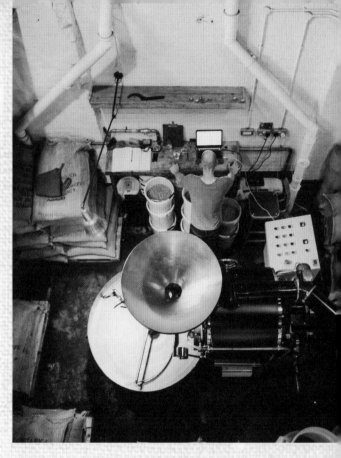

ABOVE It's no secret that recording and referencing roast data is the pathway to delicious results.

coffee bean to jettison moisture stores. Worse still, the breakdown of sucrose (sugar) and the subsequent caramelization that occurs from 150°C/300°F and upwards, releases more water, as well as carbon dioxide, as by-products. The water turns to steam, which in turn, along with a build-up of carbon dioxide, places increasing amounts of pressure on the physical structure of the bean. Something has to give, and without the plasticity that water once provided, the enlargement becomes more brutal. And like a snail whose shell has become too small to contain it – the consequences are explosive. This stage of the roast is known as 'first crack' and it is marked by an audible popping sound reminiscent of snapping pencils and an immediate increase in the size of the bean. First crack typically occurs after 7–9 minutes in a drum roaster (some air roasters can get there in only 2–3 minutes when pushed to it) and it can

can be risky as they shine a very revealing light on green coffee, readily exposing any off-notes or defects. But when the green coffee is of very high quality and the roaster knows how to handle it, these light roasts gloriously stretch the limits of coffee's flavour profile into heady heights of fruitiness. Coffee this light is best suited for filter brewing or French press, and almost always too light (and acidic) for espresso brewing.

As the roast pushes on beyond first crack, things begin to move faster. Whereas in the early stages of roasting colour development and aroma shifted more deliberately, now the progress must be monitored closely, as important physical and chemical changes are occurring by the second. The plant cell walls of the bean become fractured, denatured and more brittle. The voids left by the quickly departing water begin to expand faster, which in turn, makes the bean more porous. Oils begin to migrate around the structure of the bean, too.

During this time, the subsequent flavour of the coffee will be changing constantly as well. Acidity drops off more or less linearly throughout the roast and bitterness increases exponentially through caramelization effects, while the more elusive attributes of body and sweetness increase, plateau, then drop off again – exactly when that happens is down to the coffee and the whims of the roaster, of course.

If there's a first crack, it stands to reason that there must be a second crack (otherwise it would be known only as just 'crack', I suppose), and this second audible phase normally commences around 2–5 minutes after first crack finishes. Most speciality coffee is dropped into the cooling tray at some time between first crack and second crack, but darker roasts that may be used for espresso brewing will sometimes dip into later stages during, or after, second crack. Second crack is harder to hear than first crack and once again, we are looking at a build-up of carbon dioxide within the bean, but by this time almost all of the water has gone.

After second crack, tensions become high. Things are beginning become reminiscent of a

last from 30–120 seconds, when the average temperature of the bean sits at around 190°C/375°F.

First crack is more than just an audible checkpoint. It's also a marker for a significant physical change in the dynamic of the roast as a whole. Up until just before first crack, the coffee has been drawing in energy from the hot roasting air and, if available, the metal surfaces of the roaster itself. First crack, however, is like a firework going off inside the roaster, and the rapid phase change of water into steam creates a temperature hike as the bean itself gives out heat energy (becomes exothermic) for a short time. Anticipating first crack is an important skill for a roaster, as the sudden change in energy dynamics can cause the roast to 'run away' and get too hot or, if insufficient energy is provided, it stalls.

Once first crack has finished, the coffee can be considered roasted and fit for consumption. Coffee this light will usually be bright and fruity, exhibiting far more of the beans natural facets and less in the way of traditional 'roast' qualities. Lighter roasts campfire by now, in both sound and smell, at least. At temperatures above 230°C/450°F, the matrix structure of the plant begins to deteriorate. The aromatic lignin (essentially nature's cement) begins to volatize, which threatens the stability of the bean but also opens up new aromatic potential in the realms of nutty, smoky and charred flavours. As the roast becomes even darker, the coffee starts to burn.

Perhaps only 15 minutes have passed, and the beans have nearly doubled in size, yet lost over 20 per cent of their starting mass, which equates to a drop in density of almost 50 per cent. The character of coffee at this late stage in the roast has been all but obliterated; sooty, astringent and bitter caramel flavours have taken over. Oils begin to bleed onto the surface of the bean and the roast emits a darker, more ominous smoke. Continuing roasting beyond this point would be both pointless – since the coffee is likely already undrinkable – and more importantly, dangerous. Just before the beans reach their ignition point they turn as black as coal. Then the roaster catches on fire.

ROAST PROFILING AND TEMPERATURE GRAPHS

So there is far more to roasting than setting a heat dial and a countdown timer. A coffee's roast profile can be based on a number of factors, including bean density, coffee variety, origin and type of processing. It may also be based on the intended brewing method of the roasted coffee. Roasting is a highly sensitive process where even the smallest shift in variables can have monumental repercussions in the chemistry of the coffee, ultimately affirming the character and quality of the finished coffee bean.

Thinking of the coffee bean like a checklist of flavour compounds can help to demystify the roasting process. Each flavour, or group of flavours, will only become apparent, or slip away, once a specific bean temperature has been achieved and maintained for a period of time. Some flavour compounds decrease as roasts get darker and others increase. Nicotinic acid, for example, is one contributor to a clean finish in a good cup of coffee, and it is present in higher quantities in dark roasts due to the action of higher temperatures releasing its soluble form. Other flavour groups may remain relatively stable, but their presence might be suppressed or made more noticeable by the increase or decrease in other aromatic compounds.

The best coffees are roasted to specific profiles, where temperature is regularly adjusted to coerce the roast along, or to slow down its progress. Profiles are recorded in graph form, with axes that track the air temperature and bean mass temperature, resulting in a visual record and a useful reference of the roasters approach to the task at hand. Some modern roasters are capable of memorizing the actions of a roaster during a roast, then repeating the exact same steps on subsequent roasts for consistent batch-to-batch results.

One of the most important ways that a temperature graph can help a roaster is through its recording of the Rate-of-Rise (RoR). The temperature of the coffee bean during any roast should always be on the increase, but most experts agree that the speed at which the temperature increases should occur at a decreasing rate. That is, the rate of rise should decrease through the course of the roast – think of it like a car that is slowly decelerating, but still constantly moving forward. This has to do with inner bean development. Simply put, it's more likely that a coffee will taste good when it is the same colour on the inside as the outside. The bean will always be slightly less cooked on the inside than the outside however, due to the nature of conductive heat. To mitigate this fact, roasters aim to increase bean temperature rapidly at the beginning of the roast, then more slowly at the end. The effect is a curious game of catch-up, where the interior temperature of the bean lags behind at first (as the heat has had insufficient time to conduct through) then rapidly increases a minute or two later, thanks to the initial temperature blast. By that time, the RoR on the exterior of the bean has slowed down and the inner and outer temperatures sit in close proximity to one another.

Careful manipulation of the rate of rise, mostly through the control of temperature and airflow, is where the hand of the roaster comes into play.

ROASTING COFFEE AT HOME

Home coffee roasters can be picked up for as little a £200/$315 and what some of them lack in control and stability they make up for in the fact that you have freshly roasted coffee on tap. With a little trial and error these machines can produce surprisingly good results, and more expensive roasters can even match the quality of output that commercial models achieve.

Temperature control is everything in roasting. Most home roasters come with a panel that controls this digitally, and some have the function to programme a temperature curve so that the same roast can be repeated. The controller for this is paired with a temperature probe that usually takes a reading from the metallic surface on the inside of the drum, or from the temperature of the air being blown in. These temperatures are useful because they tell you how the roaster heats up, but this is only truly relevant when they're paired with a temperature reading from the beans themselves (bean mass). Most roasters do not come fitted with a probe that can do this, so I suggest buying a digital temperature probe and inserting it into the drum, or better still, connecting a USB probe to your computer or smartphone then using one of the excellent data logging apps that will record the progress of your roast. Establishing a set-up like this is surprisingly cheap and easy, but provides a level of control and evaluation that will show in your coffee.

When you're choosing where to put your roaster ventilation is one of the main concerns. If you're roasting indoors I would recommend sitting the roaster underneath the extractor hood of your oven, or at least next to an open window. Coffee roasting produces a lot of smoke, even on short roasts, and you'll not want it hanging around in your house. Better still, do it outside or in an outbuilding, which solves the smoke problem and, for those of you that live in a colder part of the world, also helps a great deal with cooling the beans once they have been dropped into the cooling tray.

Follow the roaster's instructions and pay particular attention to the recommended batch size.

Small home roasters can sometimes be very sensitive to small or large loads. Under-loading leads to inconsistent cooking (like flash-frying, the bean may be underdeveloped on the inside) and overloading slows the roast down, which in extreme cases results in woody/smoky flavours. Also locate where the chaff is collected and how it is emptied from the machine. If left to build up, chaff can cause problems with airflow and become a fire risk.

On a final note, it's important never to leave your roaster unattended – you'll not be able to enjoy the delicious fruits of your labour if your house burned down in the process. Fire risk is something that commercial roasteries take very seriously, and roasting small batches in your home should be subject to the same degree of precaution.

A

1 Preheat the roaster. It's important that the bean temperature ramps up quickly at the start of the roast, so sufficient preheating of the roaster's components is essential. Fire on all cylinders until the air temperature is at least 200°C/400°F.

2 Drop the beans in and set the timer (**A**). The bean mass probe will show a sharp temperature drop as it comes into contact with the cool beans, but after around a minute it should bottom out and then begin to increase.

3 Keep an eye on the bean mass temperature, which should be increasing rapidly, but beginning to slow its increase as you approach the eight-minute mark (**B**).

4 First crack will present itself as an audible snapping noise after around 9–12 minutes, depending on the model of the roaster. It's here that careful temperature manipulation is required to stop the beans from 'running away' if too much temperature is applied, or from 'stalling' if your roaster has insufficient heat.

5 As the beans develop after first crack the surface will become smoother and the aromas more pleasant. When you decide to finish the roast will depend on how you intend on brewing them as well as the type of coffee you are roasting. Experimenting with this is half of the fun of roasting. Having said that, if you'd like to stick to convention, most experts agree that first crack should occur at around 80 per cent of the total roast time. This means if you hit first crack at 10 minutes you should end the roast after 12 and a half minutes. You may of course wish to roast for longer. Drop the beans into the cooling tray (**C**).

6 Some home roasters do a much better job of cooling roasted coffee than others. Ideally the beans should be cool enough to handle 5 minutes after the end of the roast (**D**). Bag them up and allow to outgas for at least 12 hours.

B

C

D

THE IMPORTANCE OF ROAST DATE AND STORAGE

Freshly roasted coffee doesn't taste nice. No, really. Before you think me mad, I am not talking about coffee freshly bought from the store, but coffee fresh off the cooling tray. That stuff. This should come as no surprise. After all, the coffee has just undergone a wholly unnatural experience; moisture stores and solid matter have been vaporized; sugars and acids have splintered into a diverse mixture of newly formed chemicals; caramelization and browning reactions have ensued, and the overall structure of the bean has been dramatically transformed, resulting in a near doubling of size and changes to porosity, colour, density and weight. Brewing coffee that fresh will produce a drink that tastes flat, ashy and lifeless, with little in the way of complex aroma.

The coffee must be allowed to rest before it is ready to be turned into a tasty beverage. The most important element of resting is the process of 'outgassing', or the process of releasing carbon dioxide from the bean. Secondary to that are the minor chemical changes that also take place minutes, hours and even days following the roast.

Freshly roasted coffee is approximately two per cent carbon dioxide by weight, and if left in a non-pressurized environment, it will release this gas more slowly as time goes on. This is all down to the internal pressure of the bean which – like an inflated balloon – forces carbon dioxide and other gases outwardly after roasting. Now, carbon dioxide is flavourless by itself, but when mixed with water – in, say, a French press – the hot liquid acts an effective solvent for the carbon dioxide, which quickly dissolves in and subsequently, out, of the water, creating lots of bubbles. The effect is like pouring a glass of fizzy cola over a sherbet, and as fun as that may sound, it doesn't make for a great-tasting cup.

There are two main reasons for this. The first is that when carbon dioxide and water mix they produce carbonic acid. The subtle 'tang' that you experience from a glass of soda that has been left to go flat is the taste of carbonic acid. The point is that carbonic acid isn't very delicious, it leaves a 'licked-battery' kind of sensation on the tongue, and it can become quite apparent in very fresh brews.

It has also been suggested that carbon dioxide is bad for brewing due to the disruption it causes to the mechanics of brewing, where wet coffee grounds that are rapidly releasing carbon dioxide have the effect of propelling brewing water away from the flavourful solubles that rest within the hallowed inner walls of the coffee cell structure. The result is a less complete extraction (for more on extraction see pages 69–71).

The amount of time that coffee must be allowed to rest and outgas will depend on the approach to roasting and storage. Broadly speaking, darker and hotter roasts will have a higher internal pressure, so will they will outgas slightly quicker and more completely. Lighter and cooler roasts will do the opposite. Faster outgassing points towards a more porous bean structure, which is also more likely to go stale quickly (see below). It would seem that a direct correlation can be made between the rate and extent of outgassing and the volatilization (departure) of aromatic compounds in the first week or so after roasting. A coffee's aroma tends to be more noticeable in lighter roasts; in darker roasts, the destruction of volatile aromatics (or at least the good ones) eventually outpaces the formation.

FRESHNESS AND STALENESS

The inevitable deterioration in coffee quality after roasting remains an inconvenient truth that, sadly, too many people choose to ignore. While some of the mechanisms responsible for staleness can be limited through packaging and correct technical processing, they cannot be entirely stopped. Typified by a loss of aroma and general muddying of flavour, staleness can be largely attributed to the departure of aromatic molecules and oxidation reactions. We experience this escape of aromatic volatilization every time we open a bag or box of coffee beans or even smell a coffee shop on the other side of the street!

Oxidation is a destructive action, responsible for the discolouring of fruit and vegetables and the eventual rancidity of fats and oils. In the case of coffee, oxygen molecules, present within the air, lend electrons to compounds and transform them into new oxidized compounds. The loss of positive flavour molecules and the creation of new, generally inferior (from a taste standpoint) compounds, presents itself as an overall loss of flavour.

The rate of oxidation in coffee is largely proportionate to its rate of outgassing. Very fresh coffee actually oxidizes quite slowly, since the internal bean pressure prevents too much oxygen gaining access. Inevitably, though, as the rate of out-gassing drops, oxygen finds its way in. There are other factors at play, too; oxidation is increased by air humidity, for example. Storing coffee in a cool and dry environment still remains one of the best and simplest ways to preserve freshness.

At some point during the exodus of aroma and the effects of oxidation, coffee crosses a threshold of acceptable loss and is eventually deemed to be too old and stale to be enjoyable. As for when exactly the coffee is at its peak level of performance, there are only broad guidelines. Certainly it takes at least 12 hours for the coffee to become drinkable, and in some cases up to a week to reach its full potential. It may be that not all oxidation effects are detrimental to coffee quality and that not all aromatic losses are actually a loss. The variables are too numerous to give even vaguely specific guidelines on when best to use your coffee, but assuming the coffee is stored correctly, I would advise using filter coffee within 1–10 days of roasting and espresso within 7–14 days.

PACKAGING AND PRESERVATION

There are a variety of packaging options, and which one is best for you will be determined by how you intend on using the coffee. Whichever method you use, keeping coffee in an unsealed container is not a clever move as it will leave coffee wide open to staleness. Coffee stored like this should be consumed within 1–2 days.

Valve bags are the most common method of packaging for most commercial roasters. The valve allows the steady release of gases generated during roasting and the containment of aroma. Since carbon dioxide is steadily leaking out, it becomes difficult for oxygen to get in, meaning that the

airspace of the bag is effectively flushed with carbon dioxide. I have seen some data that suggests the airspace in a valve bag may consist of as much 50 per cent carbon dioxide in only five minutes after loading freshly roasted coffee. Once opened, oxygen is of course introduced, but assuming the bag is sealed again it is eventually flushed out again. Some roasters take the extra step to flush their bags with nitrogen when filling them, eliminating any oxidation effects until the bag is eventually opened. Vacuum-sealing a valve bag achieves the same thing.

Valve bags do not prevent outgassing, however, and since the level of outgassing is relative to the bean's internal pressure, which is also relative to the menacing potential of oxidation, freshly opened bags of three-week-old coffee, for example, will go stale very quickly.

One workaround would be to store the coffee in a pressurized container. Also, freezing remains a simple and fairly effective method for the long- and short-term preservation of roasted coffee. I have been, for some years now, freezing carefully measured individual portions of roasted coffee to great effect. Be sure to freeze in sealed bags or containers, though, to avoid moisture condensing onto the surface of the beans.

BELOW Bagging coffee quickly after roasting limits its contact time with oxygen.

THE SCIENCE
AND FLAVOUR
OF COFFEE

04

HOW FLAVOUR WORKS

The subject of coffee flavour chemistry is broad enough to warrant a book many times the size of this one, never mind a section of these humble proportions. Over 300 flavour constituents have been identified in green coffee to date, rising to around 900 in the roasted coffee bean through the formation of new aromatic molecules. In isolation these compounds each possess unique smell and taste properties, but their interaction with one another may form countless new aroma sensations.

Traditionalists will argue that the success of a brewed cup of coffee should be measured in its enjoyment. Are the character traits of the coffee reflected in the cup? Are there defected or off-notes in the character of the coffee itself? Is the extraction balanced, not too bitter and not too bright? Is there sweetness in the cup and does the flavour feel 'clean'? The human body has reached a state of rare perfection when it comes to analysing the stuff we put in our mouths. There is no instrument, man-made or otherwise, that is capable of achieving the multifunctional feats of the human oral and olfactory system. You don't need expensive equipment or a chemistry degree to answer these questions; drinking coffee regularly can make anyone an acceptable judge of cup quality.

But (and it's a big but) in cafés and at home, it's nice, if not essential, to be able to repeat great results over and over again; the rituals that we develop to make our favourite brews ('infuse for this long', 'dose that much', 'stir for 20 seconds with this spoon') aim to do this. Some of us are happy with the results that we achieve as long as they remain consistent; the knowing why is secondary to the hassle-free enjoyment of a good cup. But for many of us, the pursuit of perfection demands a greater understanding of why different practices produce different results, because it's the understanding why, that can unlock the secrets of how to make that great cup even better.

SWEETNESS

Sweetness is a confusing concept when it comes to coffee. On the one hand, it is estimated that over 50 per cent of coffee drinkers in the UK (and around 35 per cent in the US) add sugar to their coffee, but on the other hand we use words like 'caramel', 'chocolate', 'nougat' and 'brûlée' to describe an unsweetened cup.

A roasted coffee bean comprises approximately 0.2 per cent *sugars*, a relatively small amount by itself, and even smaller once brewed with water, meaning that a typical cup of French press coffee is only around 0.06 per cent *sugars*. I place the word *sugars* in italics, since we are not necessarily talking about the everyday white granules that come in a bag, but other long-chain polysaccharides that exhibit some sugary characteristics, but with far less actual sweetness than the type of sugar we are familiar with.

A cup of coffee is not inherently sweet, but familiar 'sweet' aromatics created during roasting (see pages 54–57), coupled with trace amounts of complex sugars and caramels, give a perception of sweetness in the cup. A higher viscosity, i.e. thickness in the cup, likely amplifies this perception, too.

I personally see sweetness as an excellent objective for any kind of coffee brewing, with it seeming to peak at just the moment where all other contributing forces balance perfectly.

BITTERNESS

Bitterness is commonly used as a scapegoat for all manner of imperfections in a brew. For many of us, if a coffee tastes bad, it's because it's bitter. This is a little unfair, however, since the sensation which we describe as bitterness is often that of astringency or sourness, and in the case of espresso-based drinks the source of bitterness comes not from the coffee itself, but from overcooked (or 'burnt' milk).

Two compounds, trigonelline and quinic acid (the same stuff that provides tonic water with its bitterness), are thought to contribute much of the bitterness in coffee. Caffeine, though assumed to be flavourless, actually tastes bitter too (see page 66).

By itself, bitterness is an unpleasant sensation, but it can do a great job of focusing sweetness and taming acidity when balanced correctly. It's the structure that bitterness offers that brings order to the other elements of a cup of coffee.

The presence of bitterness in the cup is often down to overextraction of the coffee. This means that a very slow espresso extraction, or a very long French press brew will produce a more bitter coffee. Likewise, a very quick extraction will exhibit low levels of bitterness. The grind size, brewing temperature and water (see pages 68–69) will also affect this, as will the darkness of the roast, since darker roasts have a higher solubility and in turn produce a more bitter cup. It seems plausible that bitter compounds are slower to extract than those of sweetness and acidity, but once they do come through, it is easy for them to dominate a cup.

ACIDITY

Acidity might sound scary, but it is a very important element in a good cup of coffee, providing fruitiness, juiciness, roundness and one of my favourite features: refreshment! Those at the early stages of coffee discovery often find it quite surprising how clean, grippy acidity can set apart a cup of well-brewed coffee from what they might be used to.

High-acidity coffees tend to be grown at higher altitude and tend to have undergone the fully washed processing method (see pages 30–31). Some coffee producers, from countries like Kenya and Colombia, have built a reputation for producing bright, acidic coffees.

There are many different acids in roasted coffee, but the most abundant are citric (also found in citrus fruits), malic (also found in apples), lactic (found in dairy products) and acetic (vinegar). However, the concentration of acids within a cup of coffee is not an accurate gauge of acidity, since the buffering effect of salt, as well as the presence of bitterness and sweetness can all skew our perception of acidity.

A study by the Technical Unit of the International Coffee Organization in 1991 showed that grind size, brew time and brew temperature all have an effect on extraction of the 30 or so acids in roasted coffee. As you would expect, a finer grind produces a slightly more acidic coffee, but with increasingly higher temperatures and longer brew times, the concentration of acids peaks before 100°C/212°F and 14 minutes, respectively. What this means is that with very long brews and very high-temperature brews, some acids are denatured or destroyed altogether, reducing their overall concentration.

The acid concentration, or pH, of roasted coffee changes through the course of the roast. Green coffee generally has a pH of around 5.8, which drops to approximately 4.8 on or around the time of first crack.

AROMA

The concept of aroma is not limited to the simple act of smelling coffee as it wafts over towards us. Retronasal smell, or the smell that we experience as we breathe out through our noses when holding a mouthful of coffee is also a hugely important factor. Once combined with the sensory input from the tongue concerning taste, texture and temperature (as well as other stimuli), the brain is able to devise an accurate representation of the coffee, these are slight chemical changes in our grey matter, but a powerful emotive experience to our consciousness.

If you've ever held a drink in your mouth while holding a thumb and finger over your nose, you'll have found that flavour is pretty boring when the nose isn't involved. It is the hundreds of volatile aromatics in coffee interacting with the olfactory epithelium (one of the specialized types of tissue) in our noses that gives us the larger chunk of a coffee's flavour profile.

The breadth and complexity of such things is certainly beyond my own understanding, and superfluous to the scope of this book. But in summary, many of the aromatic qualities that we associate with a cup of coffee come from the furan family (aromas including toffee and bran), pyrazine family (aromas such as earthiness, vegetal, walnut), and thiazole family (aromas like toast, nuts and brown meat).

A good set of scales (or even three) will quickly become your best friend on the journey to tasty coffee.

With that in mind, if you take a flick through the later pages of this book, you'll see that almost every brew method and recipe calls for ingredients to be weighed rather than measured. It might feel awkward at first, but I promise that once you get used to it, you will never look back – and that goes for cooking, too.

A WORD ON IMPERIAL AND METRIC

I have become increasingly disenchanted with the imperial system over the past years for a number of reasons. Firstly, pints, cups, pounds and ounces fall very short of the mark when it comes to precision measurement, with some areas of coffee requiring measurements in $1/100$ of an ounce. Secondly, the metric system is also vastly superior in its ability to scale measurements by only changing the prefix – 140 g is equal to 0.14 kg, for example – and calculating brew ratios.

I recommend acquiring two sets of digital scales (although it is possible to get by with only one): one for measuring small quantities of coffee grounds (this scale should have increments of 0.1 g) and one for measuring larger quantities, such as water in a pour-over brew (this scale will get by with 1 g increments but should be capable of measuring up to 5 kg). Scales needn't be expensive – both sets should cost you no more than £30/$47, but do read the reviews. Also note that scales need to be serviced from time to time to keep them on the money, so get a set of calibration weights for this.

THE SIGNIFICANCE OF SCALES

I think it goes without saying that taking time to accurately measure and record your adventures in coffee will make for tastier brews and improved consistency in the future. Working with digital scales instead of measuring jugs/pitchers or spoons helps this process as it's faster, more precise, less messy and requires no additional equipment. Scales are actually a more appropriate way of measuring things for all areas of culinary arts, but in the case of coffee they are notably of great use when directly comparing the mass of solids and liquids for brew ratio and extraction yield calculations (see pages 69–71). And indeed, a good set of scales has never been more imperative than in the minefield of espresso coffee, which presents challenges when attempting to do things without scales and by volume alone, since the dissolved gases that are part and parcel of the nature of the brewing method can give the illusion of a larger volume of liquid than is actually the case.

CAFFEINE

The term 'caffeine' was originally coined by the German chemist F. F. Runge in the mid-19th century. The word itself is conjunction of the German *kaffee* (coffee) and the chemical suffix *-ine*. The French translated it to *caféine* and, in turn, the English caffeine. An alkaloid (a naturally occurring chemical compound, many of which are stimulants), caffeine, is designed to be a natural deterrent against insects, but I suppose the added bonus is that larger animals (who readily digest coffee beans and prepare them for germination) seem to love the stuff. Almost all plants containing mind-altering alkaloids are grown in the tropics, where the competition for survival is so fierce that the plants have developed increasingly elaborate ways to defend themselves. Caffeine can be found in over 60 other plants besides coffee, including tea, kola nuts, *yerba maté* (a leaf similar to tea, popular in South America), and guarana berries, to name a few – but given the word's etymological origins, it's is fair to say that the very definition of caffeine is 'coffee chemical'.

And that 'coffee chemical' is now the most widely consumed drug in the world, surpassing that of nicotine and even alcohol. *New Scientist* magazine state that around 90 per cent of North Americans consume caffeine on a daily basis (approximately 75 per cent of which is coffee). It's mankind's obsession with caffeine's stimulating effect that has led to an increasing number of consumer products containing a synthesized form of the drug, from the obvious sodas and soft drinks through to the new wave of energy drinks, as well as ice cream, gum and even shaving gel.

A 200-ml/7-fl. oz. cup of filter coffee can vary wildly in terms of caffeine content, but may typically contain around 120 mg (0.12 g) of caffeine, or 600 mg/litre. However, it is estimated that 120,000 tons of caffeine are consumed globally every year - equivalent to up to 800 billion cups of coffee. Caffeine typically accounts for between 1.2–2.5 per cent of the dry matter of green coffee and around 0.7 per cent of the dry coffee cherry. The *robusta* species has, in the past, been celebrated for its overinflated caffeine content, and this is indeed true, but evidence suggests that other growing factors, variety and processing methods also have a part to play. Recent studies seem to agree that darker roasts do cause some sublimation of caffeine molecules, which have a boiling point of 178°C/352°F, but this is offset by an overall reduction in bean weight and density, so the effect is somewhat negated. Besides, anyone selecting coffee based on caffeine content and its correlation to roast profile would be somewhat missing the point.

Since caffeine is highly soluble, the brewing technique, within reason, makes little or no difference to the caffeination of the final beverage. Of course, the brew ratio (ratio of coffee to water) will affect the mg/litre of caffeine in the final drink, and for this reason it's better to relate caffeine content to the grams of coffee that you are consuming, rather than the volume of the drink. The common belief is that caffeine is flavourless, but this is in fact incorrect. Pure caffeine has a very strong bitter flavour and even its modest presence in coffee is thought to provide around 10 per cent of coffee's bitterness – certainly enough to subtly differentiate the beverage from those absent of caffeine.

Our bodies metabolize caffeine readily and the effects can be felt almost immediately, but it typically reaches peak performance after about 30 minutes; after three hours, the effects are half what they were at the point of peak performance. It can take over 12 hours for the drug to leave your system altogether, but the exact time varies according to lots of other factors: hydration, food, exercise, smoking, alcohol, race, age and even gender. In *The World of Caffeine: The Science and Culture of the World's Most Popular Drug*, authors Bennett Alan Weinberg and Bonnie K. Bealer muse that a nonsmoking Japanese man drinking his coffee with an alcoholic beverage would likely feel caffeinated 'about five times longer than an Englishwoman who smoked cigarettes but did not drink or use oral contraceptives.'

The psychological and physiological influence that caffeine has on the brain and sympathetic nervous system is of such an acute precision that it almost seems a shame not to regularly exercise it. Caffeine first disarms the natural mechanisms that cause us to feel drowsy, and then takes command, firing neurons that stimulate the pituitary gland, raising our heart rate and causing a sudden release of blood sugars and adrenaline.

It achieves this by being chemically similar to the

molecule adenosine, which tricks neurons (nerve cells) in the brain. Adenosine appears in higher concentrations when we have expended lots of energy and clings to neurons like expanding foam, causing the slow-down of brain functions and the feeling of tiredness. Caffeine behaves like an evil-twin, however, fooling the neurons and latching on in place of adenosine. This anomaly is known as 'competitive inhibition' because the caffeine is inhibiting the effects of adenosine by competing with it for places on the neurons' adenosine-receptors.

With the impostor in place, one might think that the neuron would behave normally, but the kicker is that caffeine has the opposite effect of adenosine, and actually provokes the neuron into firing faster than usual. The pituitary gland, a pea-sized gland at the base of the brain, becomes aware of this and stimulates the sympathetic nervous system into 'fight or flight' mode – an emergency protocol that dilates the pupils, increases heart rate, and releases sugar stored in the kidneys. It's this two-pronged attack mechanism that makes caffeine such an effective stimulant.

Since as far back as the 1800s, the negative effects of caffeine in coffee have been cited by coffee's opponents, such as Charley Post, the inventor of the caffeine-free 'healthy' coffee alternative known as Postum, also known as 'America's Favorite Coffee Substitute'. Like most drugs, caffeine use (and abuse) is open to potential side-effects, along with the danger of withdrawal symptoms. Those of us who have developed a tolerance to caffeine have actually developed additional adenosine receptors – our bodies' way of giving the drowsy molecule a better chance of slowing us down when we deserve a rest. No problem if you've plenty of coffee on tap, but it can spell bad news for caffeine junkies unable to get a fix, since the adenosine will have a greater number of receptors to bind to and the feeling of tiredness can be amplified – in other words, you feel withdrawal. Very heavy caffeine consumers may even experience mood swings when deprived of caffeine, since the drug is linked to the production of serotonin, which regulates such things as mood, appetite and sleep.

Clinical trials have failed to find lasting negative effects from overconsumption of caffeine, however, but a great deal of new research seems to indicate that caffeine might be a powerful positive force in the fight against various mental illnesses. It has for some years been suggested (and subsequently proven) that caffeine slows the memory decline in old age, but more recent studies have found that moderate caffeine intake in mice prevents brain-cell deposits of a protein that is a specific hallmark of Alzheimer's. Trials also indicate that caffeine may be a powerful preventative and therapeutic drug in the fight against Parkinson's disease.

WATER

Discussing the quality of water you use in coffee normally provokes a roll of the eyes from those who have yet to discover the monumental impact it really has. Water fulfils two roles in coffee brewing: first as an ingredient, where it represents at least 90 per cent of the cup of coffee, and second as a solvent, where it is used to extract soluble flavour from ground coffee.

The first of these roles can easily be managed by a simple taste test; if your water tastes bad before you brew with it, it will almost certainly be reflected in the resulting cup. Water used to make coffee should contain no chlorine taste, so I'd advise using bottled mineral water in your kettle instead of water straight from the tap/faucet, or filtering your water before using it. Either of these steps will help to improve the flavour of your coffee.

Water as a solvent is slightly tougher to get your head around, but no less impactful in respect to cup quality. With the exception of water that has been completely demineralized, all water contains some dissolved particles and we broadly refer to this as the water's hardness; more specifically, it's calcium carbonate, also known as limescale, that is responsible. Just to give you an idea of the difference in water's hardness according to the area in which you live, I grew up in Cornwall in the rural South West of the UK, where the tap water was very soft, comprising around 70 parts per million (ppm) of total dissolved solids (TDS). I later moved to London, where the tap water is very hard – containing around 400 ppm TDS. You can buy an inexpensive TDS meter to measure your own, but TDS only tells you how much stuff is lurking in the water, not the specific chemical breakdown. Your local water supply should be able to

provide with you that information, however. Common minerals and compounds found in hard water are magnesium, fluoride, sodium, chlorine and a whole array of mineral salts. Some levels of these are acceptable, while others should be tackled with a zero tolerance policy (see the table below).

Very hard water (high TDS) seems to make a poor solvent and is therefore harder to brew with. This is probably because it already contains more soluble content and is that little bit closer to its saturation point. As a result it extracts less – or less of the desirable stuff at least – from the coffee. This would lead one to think that demineralized water makes the best brewing water, but weirdly (and I have yet to find an explanation for this), it would appear that some level of TDS (above 70 ppm, ideally) is desirable.

The SCAA (Speciality Coffee Association of America) recommends the following acceptable range for brewing water:

Total Chlorine	0 mg/litre
TDS	75–250 mg/litre
Calcium Hardness	17–85 mg/litre
Total Alkalinity	At or near 40 mg/litre
pH	6.5–7.5
Sodium	At or near 10 mg/litre

WATER TEMPERATURE

The best temperature for brewing coffee is between 90–95°C/195–205°F; the opposite ends of this scale do produce a different style of cup. Water temperature is perhaps an area of coffee geekery that has become overstated. Top-of-the-range espresso machines are now – supposedly at least – capable of adjusting the temperature of water by one-tenth of a degree, which is almost as impressive as it is over-engineered for the purpose.

It is generally accepted that darker roasts prefer the lower end of this scale, and lighter roasts prefer the higher end, which is largely to do with the higher-density (lighter roasted) bean requiring a little more coercion to give up the goods. But in an instance where a cup is not tasting quite right, I wouldn't advise anyone to tinker too much with the water temperature until all other avenues – grind size, brew ratio, brew time, water quality and coffee quality – have been explored.

To get the right temperature at home, I would advise boiling the water and leaving it to sit for two minutes, or simply adding a splash of cold water before pouring. If you have one, it's worth using a digital thermometer to check exactly if your water sits in the correct range.

EXTRACTION, STRENGTH AND BREW RATIO

Getting a handle on extraction is the key to success in every single type of coffee brewing. Badly managed extraction is the most common cause of overly bitter, sour, weak, astringent and insipid coffee. Good extraction is the source of all that is delicious in a cup of coffee; through the clarity of flavour it provides, flavour markers identifying variety, origin, processing and roast-style become evident in the finished cup. The physical extraction of the coffee gives rise to all manner of flavour-giving soluble solids and gases, along with insoluble particles of coffee fibre, proteins and oils that can contribute to the body and texture of coffee. Extraction is, not to put too fine a point on it, the singularly most important goal in coffee brewing and the common cause around which all brewing variables fight towards.

Secondary to extraction, but still of great significance, is the strength. This can be a confusing term, not least of all because we're used to seeing strength guides on jars of instant coffee, which are really trying to communicate how well-pronounced the darker elements of the coffee are. Put simply, strength is the percentage of your cup that isn't water. It might seem obvious, but mixing the appropriate amount of coffee and water (known as the brew ratio) will be the defining factor in how intense or subtle your coffee tastes, and this is one area that comes down to personal taste.

VARIABLES OF EXTRACTION

Good extraction can be achieved in a range of different brew ratios. But to do this a myriad of other factors must be considered.

Without doubt, the two factors with the most clout are the grind size and the contact time. Decrease the grind size and the surface area of the coffee increases, which increases the rate of extraction; drag out the contact time and the extraction will increase, too. Balancing these two variables, whatever the brewing method, will garner you a good footing on the path to a balanced and tasty cup. Playing with grind, dose and contact time is also a big part of the beauty of coffee brewing – discovering the unknown and creating something that has never been tasted before. For example, there is no set-in-stone way to brew an Aeropress; as long as the grind size is appropriate to the brew time, there are an infinite number of doses that will make for delicious results. Within the subject of contact we must discuss the topic of percolated coffee, or coffee made from brew water that is poured through a bed of ground beans and left to drip through a filter, which includes such brewing methods as espresso (see pages 92–95), filter (page 124–133) and to some extent siphon brewing (page 138–141) and the moka pot (page 117–119). In this scenario,

we find we find that brew ratio, grind size and brew time are all relative to one another, since the coffee acts as a barrier of resistance against the flow of liquid.

The next factor that plays an important role is brewing temperature. As with most things in the universe, the higher the temperature, the faster the reaction that takes place. In the case of coffee, this means quicker extraction at higher temperatures. There is also the matter of extraction threshold for certain compounds; caffeine, for example, extracts even at very low temperatures (under 30°C/86°F), but certain astringent compounds will only extract at near 100°C/212°F, which is why we avoid using water above 95°C/205°F.

There are other factors, too. The degree of agitation or 'turbulence' in the brewing water also affects the rate of extraction, which itself is connected to the pressure of the water, which in the case of espresso, forces itself in and out of the porous structure of the fine grounds. If you've ever needed to brew a cup of tea quickly you'd have noticed that a quick stir darkens the brew much faster than simply allowing the tea bag to hang around in the hot water. In coffee brewing a quick stir or slow agitation during brewing, or a specific ritual for pouring water and wetting grounds, can yield different results by increasing the efficiency of the brewing process. Some baristas hold their pouring technique – the stages in which water is added and the pattern in which it is poured – in almost supernatural regard. And since water can be poured in an infinite number of ways, this becomes yet another element of coffee brewing that proves difficult to communicate.

Coffee freshness can also distort an extraction, where exceptionally fresh coffee releases lots of carbon dioxide, which behaves like a force field, preventing proper contact between coffee and water. For this reason, coffee intended for espresso brewing must be rested for at least five days before brewing; otherwise the forces exerted on the coffee inside the filter basket make for a battle between gas and water where coffee is the ultimate loser. Indeed, all coffee must be rested for eight hours before it can be ground and brewed, lest the carbon dioxide upset the brewing process (see pages 60–61).

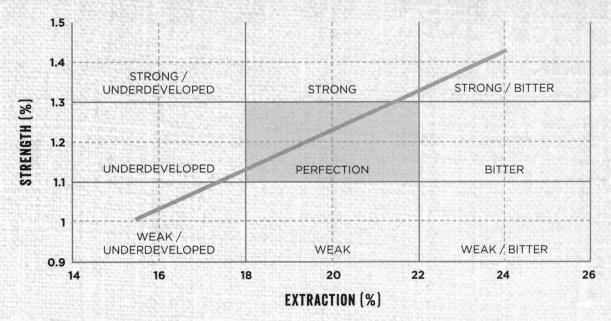

BREWING CONTROL CHART

This chart depicts the sweet spot between coffee strength and coffee extraction for non-espresso brewing methods. The vertical axis shows the strength or TDS (total dissolved solids) of the drink, expressed as the percentage that is actual coffee. The horizontal axis shows the extraction (yield) expressed as a percentage of the original dry coffee dose that has been removed by the brewing water and landed in the cup. Further down the chart, the strength of the drink decreases and at the top it is higher. For some, it may be a drink that sits closer to one of these areas that is the better one, as strength is, to some extent, a matter of personal taste. The brew ratio directly impacts beverage strength. Perfection is grey box in the centre, where the strength of the drink and the extraction percentage balance correctly (18–22% extraction and 1.1–1.3% strength) and coffee is sweeter, richer and more transparent. The diagonal grey line represents the rate of extraction and illustrates the ease in which a brew can turn out weak and underdeveloped, or strong and bitter.

BELOW In espresso brewing, the colour and persistency of the crema on top of a shot can give some clues about how successfully the coffee has been extracted.

MEASURING EXTRACTION

Extraction is best communicated as a yield percentage. What this means is the percentage of coffee (by weight) that has made its way into the brewed cup from its original dry state. It tells us how efficient the extraction process was and gives us an idea of how balanced the cup might be. The rules of extraction apply to all brewing methods, and interestingly, even though an espresso is much stronger than a filter coffee, both brewing methods should achieve about the same yield percentage; an espresso just has less water in it.

For some 50 years now, studies have been carried out to discover what percentage of the coffee used to brew with is desirable in the finished cup. Approximately one-third of the dry weight of coffee is water-soluble: i.e. it can be extracted. However, not all solubles are desirable and it's generally agreed upon by coffee professionals that an acceptable level of extraction yield sits somewhere between 18 and 22 per cent, which equates to just over half of all the solubles that are up for grabs. The extremities of this boundary define when a coffee starts to become underextracted or overextracted. In underextraction (below 18 per cent), the coffee is typically sour, thin, weak and flat. In overextraction (above 22 per cent), the coffee becomes bitter, ashy and astringent. I might add that this narrow margin for error was not simply dreamed up, but is based on the sensory analysis of hundreds of brewed coffee samples compared by coffee research panels. The rules can be bent, though, as often it will be the specific coffee and its style of roast that will dictate the best yield in the cup. For example, some coffees can excel around 16 per cent, which brings out bright, clean, fruity characteristics that would otherwise be expressed as jammy, sweet-shop notes if brewed around the 20 per cent mark. In the past, it has been suggested that coffee peaks at two distinct yields: first at around 16 per cent, then later around the broader 20 per cent mark, and that 17–18 per cent should be avoided. It's not understood why tastiness drops off between the two peaks, but I compare it to the Manhattan cocktail, which is delicious both dry and sweet, but tastes bland anywhere in-between. Sometimes we just like things one way or the other.

You can work the yield percentage out at home by weighing your coffee before brewing (which should be standard operating procedure anyway), then drying the spent coffee after brewing in a low temperature oven and weighing it again. Calculate the difference between the two samples, then divide it by the weight of the original coffee dose and you will have your percentage expressed as a decimal. Of course it'll take a few hours and it's not a particularly accurate way of doing things, so if you have a bit of money to spend, invest in a coffee refractometer (the one manufactured by VST Labs is a good option). A refractometer takes a digital reading of the brewed coffee by bouncing light through a 2 ml/^{1}/$_{16}$ fl. oz sample of cooled coffee. It's then able to determine the total dissolved solids (TDS) in the cup and, using a conversion chart, determine the solubles' yield from the coffee. Clever and useful stuff, but it'll cost you about £500/$782 for the privilege.

BREW RATIO

The other important factor to monitor during brewing is brew ratio. This number indicates the likely strength of the final cup by expressing the weight of the coffee compared to the weight of the drink. The brew ratio of an espresso usually sits at around 1.5:1, meaning that the drink is 1.5 times the weight of the coffee used to make it. This could be a 20 g/^{3}/$_4$ oz dose of coffee that is used to make a 30 g/1 oz espresso. A typical French press brew is more likely to be 15:1, where 20 g/^{3}/$_4$ oz coffee is used to make a 300 ml/10 fl. oz beverage. Remember that these calculations must be made using the beverage weight, not the weight of brew water used, on account of the coffee holding back some of the water through absorption – approximately 2 g/^{1}/$_{16}$ oz per 1 g/^{1}/$_{32}$ oz coffee.

You might be wondering where taste comes into all of this. It's easy to let graphs and formulas get in the way of the good old human tongue and nose, which constitute not only a far more sensitive system than any digital refractometer, but are also the ultimate deciding factor in whether a cup is deemed good or not. Let your mouth tell you what tastes good, and when it does, record everything you can that got you there. Much of this seems like measuring art by using science, but mastering the variables at the highest level only becomes a realistic proposition when these things are approached with respect for both the art and the science involved.

CUPPING COFFEE

Coffee cupping is a tasting practice that is used to systematically evaluate a selection of coffee samples. It is customary for cupping to take place on a long table, decked out with 6–8 cupping bowls, in which various coffee grounds and water will be smelled and tasted in a quiet, ritualistic fashion.

Cupping is a very useful tool for rapidly comparing coffees from different farms, varieties, processing methods, and for comparing different roast profiles on the same coffee, and is an invaluable practice for coffee roasters. Even though every cupping table has its own method of doing things, it has become more or less standardized across the industry, with the layout of the table and etiquette engineered to remove as many variables from the coffee brewing and tasting process as possible, so that each bowl of coffee is sampled in the same way.

The only equipment needed to conduct coffee cupping is hot water, a grinder, cupping bowls (or just a wide-rimmed cup, but bear in mind its size as you'll need to plan to use 1 g/$^1/_{32}$ oz of coffee for every 17 ml/$^3/_5$ fl. oz of capacity) and a cupping spoon (or any large round spoon).

Each cup has the appropriate dose of coarse filter-ground coffee added it to, and guests are invited to smell the dry coffee. Next the water is poured on. I prefer not to use scales for this part, as it is a bit fiddly and the trick is to get the water on top of all the samples as quickly as possible, then get your nose in there. Fill to the top of each cup, start a timer, then take in a good breath through your nose.

After taking time to nose all of the samples, it is time for the 'break'. This is usually done around four minutes after the initial pour, mirroring the parameters of a French press brew. Cuppers use the bowl of their spoon to fracture the floating raft of coffee crust that gathers on the surface, releasing aroma from the water below. More smelling ensues, followed by a period of reflection and note-taking, which is then followed by the scooping of the grounds, foam and other crud from the surface of the cup. Then, after nearly ten minutes, the coffee is tasted, an event marked by a cacophony of loud and awkward slurping noises. The purpose of slurping is to introduce as much air in to your mouth as possible, which helps promote proper aroma dispersion. In this practice, cuppers dip their spoons into the cup and scoop up a small sample of the coffee, then move it to their lips and loudly inhale.

Tasting typically goes on for another ten minutes, allowing cuppers to sample the coffee at a range of temperatures. Tasting cold coffee can also uncover defects in both the bean and the roast that may not have been apparent when the coffee was hot.

BELOW A typical cupping table, littered with spoons, beans, notes, and, of course, cups of coffee.

05

GRINDING

INTRODUCTION

In the most basic sense, grinders take coffee beans and break them up into smaller pieces. Coffee cannot be brewed as whole beans, and the increase in surface area provided by smaller particles allows better access to the inner sanctum of the bean's porous structure. The smaller you go, the more the bean's surface is exposed, which means flavour is extracted faster. Put simply, if you grind finer, the brewing time is decreased; if you grind coarser, brewing time increases.

The grinding of coffee also marks a significant point of no return in the brewing process as, once ground, the coffee is more exposed and vulnerable to the effects of oxidation, and so it remains potent only for a brief spell. If you want to make better coffee at home, probably the best piece of advice that I can give you is to grind it fresh; it is no exaggeration to suggest that doing so will produce a dramatically improved drink when compared with a cup made from pre-ground beans.

Taking this a step further, I would advise you buy the best grinder that you can afford. A good grinder will last years, require less in the way of tweaking and adjustment, and consistently produce better-tasting drinks. You see, chopping up coffee beans might seem like only a minor part of making a tasty beverage, a basic but necessary step before the real skill of brewing comes into play, but shoddy work at this early stage of coffee's precarious journey has big consequences later down the line.

HISTORY OF THE GRINDER

Before the grinder there was the pestle and mortar. Both the Arabs and Ottomans highly revered a good pestle and mortar; wear was a sign of quality and very old and well-used examples could fetch incredibly high prices at markets. For a long time, it did the job just fine, but sooner or later basic mechanical mills were invented, probably in the 12th or 13th century, although it's unlikely that they were intended for the sole purpose of grinding coffee. Consisting of little more than a dome-shaped stone that fits snugly inside a concave bowl, they were basically a mechanized pestle and mortar with a handle to affect the grinding action.

The first purpose-built mills with moving metal parts probably emerged from Syria, specifically Damascus, in the 16th century. Damascus has a long history of making sharp metal objects, including its renowned toughened steel swords and knives which, along with coffee grinders, spread through the Ottoman Empire and beyond. These early grinders were honed in Turkey, where coffee drinking was especially popular. Turkish coffee grinders first made an appearance in the mid-17th century, and this early design set the blueprint for manual grinders for the following 250 years. Indeed, examples from this era aren't dissimilar to today's small manual mills that function as handy travel companions.

These early Turkish grinders comprised two chambers, one on top of the other. Whole beans were placed in the top chamber and a handle was turned, milling the coffee and depositing it into the bottom chamber. The cutting implement in these devices was a precursor to the conical burr set, consisting of a stationary serrated hoop with a bevelled cone-shaped piece that fit closely inside. The cone would be mounted on an axis with a perpendicular handle connected at the top, which could be turned by hand to mill the coffee.

The Turkish grinder later evolved into the French and English 'lap' mills, which worked under the same principles and usually collected the ground coffee in a wooden box with a draw for easy removal. One of the earliest European references to a coffee mill comes from 1665, when Nicholas Brook, 'living at the Sign of the Frying-pan in St. Tulies-Street,' London, advertised that he was 'the only known man for making of Mills for grinding of Coffee powder, which Mills are sold by him from 40 to 45 shillings the Mill.' Many variations of the same theme appeared in the 18th and 19th centuries. Some grinders were designed to fix to a table, while some effectively were a table; others were handheld, eventually becoming wall-mounted.

The design of the cutter also evolved through this period, its evolution restricted only by the physical manufacturing capabilities of the time. At first, the early conical-style burr was cast with rough diagonal notches, but early 20th-century designs show lathe-cut pieces with two or three different teeth sizes of teeth. These models marketed themselves as being quieter, but it's likely that they also showed good improvements to the uniformity of the grind size and the effort required to get there, too.

Despite all this progress in grinding technology, it's surprising to learn that the humble pestle and mortar was still held in very high regard right up to the mid-19th century. There can be no greater testament to this fact than the written approval of Jean Anthelme Brillat-Savarin, who conceded in his *Physiology of Taste* (1825) 'the unanimous opinion was that coffee which had been beaten in a mortar was far better than that which had been ground'. It would appear that 19th-century baristas were not bereft of a certain sense of sentimentality.

The first flat burr grinders have their roots in a coffee mill patented by Thomas Bruff, Sr. in 1798. The device used two fairly flat three-inch discs with large and small cutting teeth to mill the coffee down to size. For his troubles, Bruff , who actually worked as President Thomas Jefferson's dentist (in addition to his job as a part-time coffee enthusiast) was actually granted the first U.S. patent for a coffee grinder.

Adjustable grinders began to emerge through the early 19th century, and the American market in particular embraced them. American grinders of the time tended to be both of a larger capacity than European models and more numerous, reflecting the nation's love for coffee in its early years. At the turn of the 20th century, the coffee grinder was, beyond all doubt, an indispensable piece of kitchen equipment across most of the US and Europe.

The move towards motorized grinders (for a short time powered by steam but later on becoming electrical) made a coffee grinder a sound investment for the family home, since it could grind much finer, which people took as a sign that less coffee would be needed to make a brew. Mostly manufactured in Germany and France, the first machines for use at home appeared in the 1920s and were little more than manual grinders attached to a motorized belt. Operating at only 80–100 rpm (revolutions per minute), they would have been capable of grinding

ABOVE I'd highly recommend investing in a good grinder, as it will lead to much tastier drinks.

no more than 1 kg/2.2 lbs of coffee every 15 minutes! These clunky contraptions quickly blossomed into electrical artefacts of classic candy-coloured Bakelite, and some models even had two separate hoppers: one for grinding the Sunday-best coffee and the other for grinding lower-quality beans that had been padded out with malt or peas. The introduction of paper-filter coffee in the 1930s helped create a market for electrical grinders in the home, but pre-ground coffee and instant (soluble) coffee both emerged around the same time. Soluble coffee offered a more convenient, reliable, cheap and modern take on the coffee experience, and following on from the instant coffee of World War II, it quickly became the expedient method of

HOW GRINDING WORKS

Grinding coffee is an altogether violent process, which takes its toll on the bean and eventually the grinder itself. Razor-sharp slabs of forged steel or toughened ceramic spin at 12,000 rpm, pulverizing, cutting, smashing and crushing coffee beans, before unceremoniously spitting the surviving fragments out for brewing. Heat generated during the process can damage coffee oils and can denature the fragile aromatics before they have a chance to make it into the cup. Factors like humidity, ambient temperature, roast degree and even bean density also play their part in how a grinder must be calibrated. To better understand how these factors can be mastered and what the best practices are for getting the most out of your grinder, we must first look at how coffee grinders work.

ABOVE A conical burr set can be seen at the top left of this picture, along with some flat burr variants.

coffee preparation in many countries, including the UK and the US.

On a commercial level, much bigger grinders were conceived towards the end of the 1800s to meet the needs of large-scale roasters and retailers, and eventually even those who were manufacturing soluble coffee. Roller-style mills appeared in Germany with our old friend the Jabez Burns Company releasing its 'Granulating Mill' in 1872. Descendants of this type of grinder continue to service large-scale applications even today, and at the highest end they can process many tons of coffee in an hour.

Higher-output grinders have generated new problems with overheating and clogging up, however. In response to this, manufacturers used larger burr sets to better dissipate heat, later on incorporating water-cooling into their designs. It would be these themes of heat and output that would drive the developments of grinder manufacturers through the 20th century, right up to present day.

BLADE GRINDERS

There are some machines that masquerade as coffee grinders, but would be better put to use making a fruit smoothie. They are, in almost every way, no different to a blender, and the problem with a grinder like this lies in its tendency to smash coffee beans into inconsistently sized pieces, which ultimately makes for inconsistent extraction and sourness and bitterness in the cup. While blade grinders are a better option than buying pre-ground coffee, it's far better to spend a little extra and get a burr grinder.

BURR GRINDERS

The burr grinder is made up of either two close-fitting rings that have a series of angled cutting teeth notched into them, or a conical-shaped cutter that sits inside a ring of teeth. Burr grinders produce a more uniform grind size than blade grinders, which is good news for extraction. Burr grinders are available in both electrical and inexpensive manually operated models.

The burrs must be adjustable, since every family of coffee brewer has design features that call for a specific brew time and grind size. An espresso machine demands finely ground coffee because it cannot achieve the necessary pressure that true espresso requires using coarsely ground stuff, just as a French press will provide poor filtration for very fine ground coffee, meaning that coarser is better. Setting (or 'dialling in') a grinder is an exercise in calibrating the correct grind size for the brew method and brew time, which hopefully rewards you with tasty coffee.

On most grinders, the bottom burr is attached to the motor of the grinder and the top burr is moved vertically to set the fineness. Some grinders have stepped adjustment, meaning that the setting is dictated and constricted by numbered steps on the dial. Stepless grinders offer a greater degree of precision to the grind size, but that's not to say that stepped grinders are inferior; it really depends on the setting of the step itself and the scope of grind size that the machine is designed to output.

Burrs can be made from steel or ceramic. Neither is necessarily better and much depends on the intended use of the grinder. Ceramic has a lower thermal conductivity, so it takes a little longer to heat up than steel, but one could argue that steel dissipates the heat faster and cools quicker. Both steel and ceramic are prone to dulling over time, but steel tends to do so quicker, which can cause the cutting action to become more like milling. It never ceases to amaze me how much of an improvement to a cup of coffee can be achieved by simply replacing a set of burrs.

The conical-shaped burr is shaped like a dollop of whipped cream protruding from the mouth of a conger eel. As the cone spins at 300–500 rpm, it creates a kind of whirlpool effect that, along with gravity, sucks coffee beans towards the large, 'bean breaking' segments that are responsible for the initial smash-and-stab action. Even in extremely fine or extremely coarse grinds, these first 'curls' of steel or ceramic do the same thing. As the bean fragments become smaller they are granted access to the next stage of the process, where the teeth become finer and the action more of a slice and a crunch. The grade of fineness is ultimately determined by how close the cone sits to the teeth at its base.

Flat burrs consist of two rings that are slightly concave, positioned with cutting edges facing towards one another. As the bottom burr spins, the centrifugal force propels the beans towards the finer cutting teeth on the outside of the burr ring, which shoots the beans outwards towards the thin slit of space that determines the fineness setting. Flat burrs forgo the crushing action of conical burrs, creating a nibbling effect rather than a chewing action.

One good thing about conical burrs is that adjustment is slightly more precise. This is because the cutting edges are not parallel to each other like they are on a flat burr. On a flat burr, the aperture between the two plates is directly proportional to the vertical adjustment of the burr – if you adjust by 0.5 mm, the plates will simply gain or lose a distance of 0.5 mm. On a conical burr, where the cutting faces are at around 60°, vertical movement of the adjusting burr will make for a smaller degree of separation between the burrs themselves – an adjustment of 0.5 mm will only move the burrs 0.25 mm closer, for example. This is a good thing. It allows for better precision when dialling-in the grinder. This is a moot point in the case of some modern grinders, where the adjustment is geared sufficiently to make fine adjustments very easy indeed, regardless of the burr type.

UNIFORMITY OF GRIND SIZE

Uniformity is all about how similar, or dissimilar, the grind particle sizes are from each other on any given grind setting. Different-sized pieces do things at different speeds, and the general rule of thumb is that halving the size of a coffee particle increases its extraction rate four-fold. If you cooked a quail egg, a hen egg and an ostrich egg in a (large) pan of boiling water for three minutes, the quail egg would be overcooked, the ostrich egg undercooked, and the hen egg about right. The same principles apply to brewing coffee.

A broad range of grind particles is bad, as it means the very fine particles ('fines') overextract and the very large particles ('rubble') underextract. In an ideal world, every single particle of ground coffee would be precisely the same weight, and have precisely the same surface area as the next one. This pursuit of uniform grind size has been a hot topic in the speciality coffee industry for a while, with grinder manufacturers working hard to develop new ways of cutting up coffee into similar-sized pieces.

The problem lies in coffee itself, mainly in the fact that it is brittle. When a coffee fragment is cut by a grinder burr, tiny pieces of the coffee dust fracture and splinter off – an unavoidable phenomenon that tends to be worse with darker-roasted coffees. These fines, as they are known, then easily get knocked through the burrs, exit the grinder, and become a part of the brew. Most grinders are thought to produce around 10 per cent fines in a typical sample of ground coffee. Fines are the infamous scourge of poor flow rate, uneven extraction and loss of body in espresso. They also cause overextraction and sludge in immersion brews, like the French press, plus they can stall filter brews by migrating downwards and blocking the pores in paper or cloth.

Pieces of coffee bean that are larger than the average can also make their way out of the grinder. How exactly this happens is less certain, since the aperture created by the gap between the burrs should restrict the passing of larger pieces. It's my belief that grinding, by its very nature, is violent enough to squash, extrude and propel larger pieces of coffee through gaps they wouldn't normally fit through!

Ultimately, the best grinders and best burr sets will increase uniformity and limit fines and rubble in the grounds. Using razor-sharp burrs is key, as it ensures that the beans are cut correctly and that minimal heat is produced during the cutting. The current poster boy of the coffee grinder world is the £2,400/$3,750 Mahlkonig EK43 grinder. Its unique burr set produces ground coffee that is not perfect, but it's as close to perfect as we have managed to get so far.

FINENESS

The finer the grind, the higher the surface area of the coffee. Greater surface area means a quicker extraction, because the water has better access to the flavourful compounds that the coffee holds.

For percolated coffee, where water lets gravity do the work and flows through a bed of coffee, the surface area needs to be relatively high. The first reason for this is that during percolation brewing the water has a limited contact period with the coffee. It washes through, extracting flavour as it goes. The second reason is that finer ground coffee acts as a barrier of hydraulic resistance during percolation, preventing the water from washing through and underextracting. In other words, a finer grind both speeds up and draws out extraction. A coarse grind means the water flows quickly through the bed of coffee, as well as having a slower rate of extraction. Getting the right balance means fine-tuning the grinder to reach a desirable contact period between water and coffee, and a grind particle size that corresponds to that contact period.

When immersion brewing, with a French press, for example, the fineness of the grind affects only the rate of extraction, since the water and coffee contact period is determined by the person pushing the plunger. There is, perhaps, an exception where an excessively fine grind is used in a French press, leading to filter clogging, and rendering it impossible to depress fully.

One of the biggest issues that the speciality coffee industry faces is the language and communication of grind fineness. It is perhaps the most important variable in brewing a cup of coffee and yet, even now, it is impossible for me to tell you how fine or coarse to grind your coffee. It's not even possible to draw comparisons between identical models of grinder, since even minuscule deviations in the manufacture and assembly of the grinder will give rise to a subtle reworking of the grind size. In a properly equipped lab, it is of course possible to measure particle size (in microns) and to grade different samples accordingly, but for most of us this is not a day-to-day option.

In this book, I refer to different degrees of fineness in words that describe how they might be used, i.e filter grind, Turkish grind. They are ambiguous phrases, highly inexact and only a few steps away from being utterly useless – this admission alone should illustrate the severity of the situation! The table opposite, however, may go some way towards helping you understand your grinder, so that you can get the best results possible in the cup. Please do not take it as gospel, however; part of the fun of making great coffee is tinkering with the grinder and analysing the shift in flavour. Note that the table is not linear, i.e. a coarse filter (6) is not necessarily the halfway point between filter (5) and coarse (7).

GRIND SIZE	DESCRIPTION
1	**Turkish** – the finest coffee your grinder can produce without clogging up.
2	**Fine espresso** – a very fine grind, probably with some clumping.
3	**Espresso** – a fine grind, perhaps with some clumping, particularly when moulded into an espresso portafilter.
4	**Fine filter** – somewhere between a filter grind and espresso.
5	**Filter** – coffee grounds have a caster/superfine sugar texture, rather the finer powder of espresso.
6	**Coarse filter** – similar to the fineness of granulated sugar.
7	**Coarse** – immersion brewing territory, as coarse as large sea salt flakes.
8	**Very coarse** – similar to the size of rock salt pieces, this grind is only used for long immersion brews.
9	**Chunks** – large pieces of coffee shrapnel. Too big for normal brewing.

TYPES OF GRINDER

Some grinders are designed for espresso and others for coarser-ground filter or French press brewing. Espresso grinders tend to be specialists in the realms of fine grinding, allowing for very fine-tuning at the small end of the scale, which enables them to grind very fine coffee impressively well indeed. Grinders intended for grinding filter coffee operate over a much broader range of grind sizes, but tend not to go as fine as an espresso grinder. Some grinders, it seems, can fulfil both roles adequately, although I'd argue that a grinder designed for a specific purpose will generally produce better results than a jack of all trades.

Espresso grinders come in two flavours – those with a doser (a lever on a coffee grinder that dispenses ['doses'] the ground beans), and those that are doser-less. Grinders with dosers were designed so that batches of coffee could be ground all at once, then portioned into a portafilter (the handled part of an espresso machine that holds the filter basket, into which ground coffee is placed) when an order was placed. You'll recognize them as the grinders that have a paddle or lever on the side. Obviously this is not good practice, as ground coffee should never be left to sit for more than minute or so. On the face of it, the doser-less grinder would appear to be the best choice, since it has fewer moving parts and fewer places to trap coffee grounds, as well as enabling the ground coffee finds its way straight into the portafilter basket ready for brewing. However, many grinders with dosers are now equipped with timers that grind the perfect weight of coffee to order, and the barista can dose repeatedly until the dosing chamber is empty of grounds. For some this is a preferred choice, since the doser does a neat job of depositing grounds into the filter basket, as well as the fact that doser-less grinders have a tendency to spit coffee grounds out in a devil-may-care fashion, which is both a messy and inaccurate way of operating. As with many things, a lot of it comes down to personal preference.

For modern espresso grinders the dose is calibrated by a digital timer that can be set to grind for a specific period of time. Logic would tell us that this would equate to a consistent weight of coffee regardless of how coarse or fine the grinder is set. This is not the case, however, as the finer the grind gets, the slower the output of coffee (the burrs have more work to do), meaning that the adjustments are relative to one another. We are beginning to see a new breed of grinder that aims to overcome this by automatically compensating for a change in grind fineness. In the future, I hope to see espresso grinders that dose by weight, but the mechanics of such a thing are difficult to imagine, let alone engineer.

Another problem that grinder manufacturers are having slightly more success in dealing with, but one that will likely never be truly overcome, is ground coffee retention. The pathway from the burr set to where the grounds are dispensed has long been a hiding place for stray grounds to convene, and minimizing the length of this transition along with its bias for catching grounds is the focus of many new grinder designs. From a dosing perspective, this causes only minimal bother, since the pathway is likely to hold a fairly consistent mass of coffee. From the perspective of dialling in the grinder, it does present a problem, though, as the grinder must be purged of any old grounds after making adjustments, to avoid inconsistency.

Commercial grinders intended for processing filter coffee are usually much bigger and more powerful than espresso grinders. They also tend to feature larger burr sets, meaning that they can process coffee quicker without the burrs overheating. These grinders are most effective when fed with the desired weight of coffee before being set to grind until they are empty.

Grinders need to be cleaned from time to time in order to remove stale coffee oils and to keep the grind time to a minimum. You can open up the machine, remove the burrs and clean them with a toothbrush, but a much easier method is to let the grinder chew on grinder cleaning pellets. These coffee-bean-sized nuggets manicure your burrs and scrub away oils and debris. I recommend putting 50 g/1¾ oz through for every 10 kg/22 lbs of coffee.

RIGHT A perfectly formed stream of finely ground coffee falls from the doser of a top-end Mazzer espresso grinder.

06

ESPRESSO

INTRODUCTION

Ten years ago, it would have been easy to convince the average consumer that espresso (and drinks based around the espresso) is the only acceptable way to drink coffee when out of the home. It was true, after all, that espresso was riding a 50-year rolling wave of domination, shaping the coffee shops of the Western world and beyond. Indeed, when I first learned how to make good coffee I held the strong belief that coffee prepared any other way simply would not do. Baristas were generally in agreement that big, watery cups of black coffee with – heaven forbid! – absolutely no crema (see pages 96–97) were an altogether inferior product. I do look back on those days of pursuing the 'god shot' with a great sense of nostalgia, though, and it's with a sense of focused enthusiasm that I hope to discuss the subject with you, dear reader.

And focus is as good a place to start as any, since that's what espresso is really: finely ground coffee and pressurized hot water, served in concentrated form. I once heard Stephen Morrissey, the 2008 World Barista Champion, describe making an espresso as 'like looking at coffee through a magnifying glass'. I personally liken it to watching cars race through a pair of binoculars, where mastering the difficult job of following a fast-moving object will reward you with excellent clarity of the spectacle – the downside being the apparent ease with which you can miss the mark entirely.

A shot of espresso is an honest and unforgiving thing. It celebrates attention to detail by highlighting what may be excellent about a coffee, and laughs at your bad practices by tasting intensely bad. The variables may seem a small set – grind size, dosage, extraction time and beverage weight, but the margin for error is enormous. Even when all the variables are fixed through a complex balancing act, an espresso machine and grinder can still produce unexpected results and coffee that ends up down the drain.

Why then, do we bother? Wouldn't it be easier if every café just made a big pot of coffee in the morning to last the whole day? Well, part of the allure is perhaps the seemingly endless customization of the espresso that has fostered our enduring love of the espresso bar. The simple mixture of water, coffee and milk can be bought and savoured in a remarkable range of styles and options these days and we will discuss some of these in the following section (pages 100–111).

Then, there is the freshly made convenience of the whole thing. It takes little more than 30 seconds to extract an espresso, which is a great deal quicker than any other brewing method in this book. The ritual of the barista comes into this, too. Like an engine driver mastering an infernal machine, the barista moves around with practised grace – his or her actions punctuated by a sharp hisses of the steam and a low whirr of the pump. The espresso machine is an icon of the modern café, and indeed, modern life, as much a part of the coffee shop as the beer font is to the bar.

LEFT The iconic Italian espresso with its characteristic crema crown.

THE HISTORY OF THE ESPRESSO MACHINE

To better understand how the espresso machine works and what it does, we must ask ourselves why it was needed. Before the espresso machine appeared, coffee brewing was more often than not a lengthy process. Not unlike the cafés of today, people weren't at all impressed with having to wait around for something that they believed should be made available very quickly. As a result of this, the common practice in coffee shops was to brew in bulk, then either reheat, or hold the coffee over a heat source, dishing it out on demand to those awaiting their caffeine fix. Today, there are many modern pieces of equipment that satisfy this demand in a highly effective manner – though none so quickly as the espresso machine. However, in the early 20th century it meant stewed, overextracted, and insipid cups of black soot.

The only effective solution would be a brewer that could make a single cup in under a minute, over and over again. And the only way to brew coffee very quickly is to grind it much finer, increasing the surface area of the coffee grounds and therefore the contact with the brewing water. Finer grounds meant that less water was required for proper extraction, but this posed its own problems when it came to filtering the coffee back out of the liquid, since the particles of coffee were so small. A very fine filter would go some way towards solving this, but it didn't address the problem of percolation, where gravity alone would not be sufficient to make the water pass through such a tight package of grounds. The only solution was pressure. By pressurizing the brewing water, the coffee could be ground much finer still, and in itself form a restrictive barrier for the water to pass through. As such, paper and cloth filters were out of the question, since they wouldn't be capable of withstanding the forces at play. If the water pressure remained constant, the rate of extraction could be adjusted by changing the fineness of the grind and the dose of the coffee.

Although some espresso machines can now have their pressure adjusted, it is '9 bar' (nine times the pressure exerted by the earth's own atmosphere) that was the number that was finally settled upon. To put it another way, imagine a 90-m/300-ft pipe protruding vertically out of the top of an espresso machine, and that pipe being filled to the top with near-boiling water. That is the kind of force exerted by an espresso machine today.

STEAM POWER

It was the late 19th century and Europe's near-100-year love of everything steam-powered continued to puff along. Manufacturing a near-instant pressurized coffee brewer in the 19th century was not at all easy, though. Glass and metal components were not produced in the style of modern manufacturing methods, and when placed under high pressure, explosions were frighteningly commonplace.

The earliest design for a precursor to an espresso machine that I have come across is from a patent filed in 1878 by the not-very-Italian-sounding Gustav Kessel (he was German). Kessel's machine used steam pressure to force water through a small bed of coffee and even produced a blast of steam at the end to dry the 'puck' of spent coffee for easy removal. It produced a single-serve beverage, quickly and efficiently, but there was one major flaw: it was impossible to build.

It was another six years before a machine similar to Kessel's contraption was actually built. Although all we have to go on is an old patent for its design, it was an Italian entrepreneur by the name of Angelo Moriondo who, in 1884, presented a working example of his 'new steam machinery for the economic and instantaneous confection of coffee beverage' at the Turin General Exposition. This early steam-driven espresso machine worked in a similar fashion to the Pumping Percolator of the early 1820s, by using steam pressure to force water through a bed of coffee. Moriondo's machine was a much more serious piece of bar-top kit, however, and undoubtedly the earliest-known machine that controlled steam and water in two independent boilers – a hallmark of the modern espresso machine. But despite all that, Moriondo's machine did not produce single-serve espresso as we know it; it was effectively a bulk brewer that operated at a faster rate than normal – perhaps that was why he only won a bronze medal at the General Exposition. Moriondo guarded his invention jealously, though, tinkering with the design over the years following its unveiling and manufacturing only a handful of the machines for his own stores. Sadly, there are no known confirmed examples of Moriondo machines still in existence today.

The world would have to wait until 1901 for the first commercially manufactured single-serve coffee maker, and a further two years for all the teething issues to be ironed out. It was the concerted efforts of two men, Luigi Bezzera and Desiderio Pavoni (respectively the Steve Wozniak and Steve Jobs of the Italian coffee movement), who made espresso a reality. It started with Bezzera, the ideas man. Bezzera's design for his 'Giant type with double tap' was the first to use a portafilter; it was also controlled using levers, and included options for multiple brew heads. The only downside was the fact that it was heated over an open flame. Bezzera successfully built his machine, but like so many other inventors, he lacked the marketing skill to roll it out.

Enter Pavoni. In 1903, Pavoni reportedly paid 10,000 Italian lira to Bezzera for his patent, recognizing immediately the potential for such a machine, and the pair began to work on the project together. Pavoni was more than just a marketeer, however. He introduced a couple of tweaks to Bezzera's original design, namely a pressure-release valve that directed some of the steam away from the barista, and more importantly – or perhaps less so if you're a barista being blasted with a jet of hot steam – a steam wand that could effectively target some of the machine's stored-up resources to create a useful tool for heating up milk.

They called the coffee it made *cafeé espresso* as it was made quickly and on the spur of the moment, and the finished machine, called the Ideale, was presented at the Milan Fair in 1906. The Ideale was fast, but like other steam-powered machines, it could only generate a pressure of 1.5 bar – slightly above that of a home pressure cooker. This pressure wouldn't be possible to produce the level of concentration that a modern shot possesses and by current standards this was not espresso coffee.

Over the following 40 years, Pavoni and Bezzerra's design remained relatively unchanged. Other companies began producing similar steam-powered machines, but very few left Italian shores and even within Italy, they were not as commonplace as you might imagine. It took the arrival of coffee guru Pier Teresio Arduino to make that happen. Arduino began developing his own espresso machine around the same time as Bezzera and Pavoni, but his contribution to coffee was more in the marketing of the espresso than the evolution of the machine. The most well-known example of this, and perhaps the most famous piece of espresso-related marketing of all time, is a piece of 1922 Victoria Arduino Company advertising that depicts a yellow-jacketed man grabbing an espresso from a moving train. Arduino made espresso machines sexy, and early examples of his machines can still be found all over Italy today, instantly recognizable by the eagle that adorns the top.

PISTON DESIGNS

Arduino also explored the idea of using a piston operated by a mechanical screw to generate more pressure. So too did Marco Cremonese, an inventor who, in the 1930s published detailed and wide-ranging patents that covered all kinds of espresso machines that used mechanical pistons to generate pressure in place of steam. When he died in 1936, his wife, Rosetta Scosa, attempted to license her husband's designs to various different manufacturers, but to no avail.

One of those men was the Milanese café owner and all-round tinkerer Giovanni Achille Gaggia. Gaggia filed a patent in 1938 for his own 'Rotative screw piston' coffee machine and even modified a few machines to incorporate it. World War II halted further development for Gaggia, then after the war ended, his endeavours awarded him a law suit from Cremonese's widow, who successfully sued Gaggia for patent infringement. By this point, after nearly ten years of perseverance and significant cost, Gaggia had become disenchanted by the basic design and reliability of the screw piston. He went back to the drawing board and began working on a new design that did away with screw pistons altogether. And we're all glad that he did, because his next creation would be the first machine to produce the espresso that we all know and love.

Gaggia's eureka moment was in the development

so monumental and radically unique that people literally couldn't believe what they were seeing and tasting.

of his spring piston mechanism, which solved the mechanical problems associated with the screw. Gaggia's idea was to use a hand-operated lever to compress, or cock, a spring, then once the lever was released, the enormous tension in the spring causes it to expand, forcing the piston down and pushing hot water out of the chamber and through a bed of finely ground coffee.

Stiffer springs meant higher pressure, which meant finer coffee; this, in turn, meant faster, smaller drinks. In 1947, Gaggia had a working prototype of a coffee machine, the first machine recognizable as a modern-day espresso machine. Crucially, the machine operated at pressures much higher than anything that had come before. The massive force exerted by the machines resulted in a more viscous, dense and treacly type of coffee. Furthermore, it produced a layer of brown coffee cream on top of the drink, subsequently named 'crema'. His invention, not to mention the remarkable resulting coffee, was

THE ELECTRIC PUMP

Lever machines like Gaggia's are still in operation in many cafés around the world; in fact, some cafés still use lever machines, preferring the benefit of control that they offer. But there was one more milestone in the development of espresso machine design and that arrived in 1961, with the introduction of the Faema E61, invented by Ernesto Valente. The E61 was revolutionary for a number of reasons, but most notably for its electric pump, which meant no more pistons, no more reliance on the manual force of the barista, and a much smaller machine. The pump heated tap/faucet water through a heat-exchange coil inside the boiler before directing it into the group head. In addition to this innovation, the machine also circulated hot water from the boiler through the group head continuously, to better stabilize the temperature of the machine.

HOW AN ESPRESSO MACHINE WORKS

Since the middle of the 20th century, boilers, digital thermostats, pressure management and aesthetics have advanced significantly, but in many ways the espresso machine is quite unchanged from the 1960s, and as such, can be a little inconsistent. One thing that is consistent among all espresso machines, though, is the need to pressurize water for coffee brewing. The most basic way of achieving this is still with a lever-driven piston that forces water through a bed of coffee. Some levers use a spring mechanism (see page 89), while others require arm power to generate pressure to drive water down through finely ground coffee. It goes without saying that while a manual lever might offer infinite pressure-profiling possibilities and a certain romance to its operation, they do tend to have a somewhat mercurial temperament about them.

The most basic lever machines operate via a single boiler, which feeds the group head a dose of water through either steam pressure or by gravity. Steam-pressure lever machines need a higher boiler temperature than espresso would prefer, to generate the force needed to route water up to the group head. As such, temperature regulation is nigh on impossible, and on most machines of this kind the brewing temperature increases with the more shots you pull.

Gravity-fed lever systems see the boiler located above where the coffee extracts from, allowing water to simply flow down into the group head. No steam pressure is required, so the boiler can be set to a lower temperature. These machines produce a far more consistent temperature for brewing with, but they're no good for heating milk: the lower boiler pressure is insufficiently equipped to deal with the temperature and pressure requirements of a steam wand.

THE SINGLE BOILER ELECTRIC PUMP

The most simple electrically pumped machines can make espresso and steam milk, but not as well as you might like. It does it by using two thermostats (temperature controllers): one for the steam and one for the brew water. A push button is used to control

ABOVE Modern espresso machines usually have two pressure gauges; one for the steam boiler and one for the group-head pump.

which thermostat takes priority, engaging the heating element when steam is required and switching it off (to cool down the water) when you want to make espresso. It'll work ok if you're making only one or two drinks, but beyond that it becomes very frustrating waiting for the boiler to adjust itself.

If only milk and espresso didn't taste so delicious together, then the espresso machine would be a much simpler piece of equipment. The problem with both elements is that they have unique requirements. Espresso needs 90–95°C/194°–203°F water delivered at a pressure of 9 bar/130 lbs per square inch (psi). Milk on the other hand, needs a jet of steam delivered at a minimum of 100°C/212°F and at a pressure of between 0.8–1.2 bar/12–17 psi. There's little room for negotiation from either side. Furthermore, these conditions might need to be met with consistent precision, perhaps across multiple group heads, over the course of a few hours, preferably without breaking down.

HEAT EXCHANGERS VS DOUBLE BOILERS

Heat exchangers provide one solution, consisting of a steam boiler operating at high temperature with a layer of steam floating on top that can be directed to the steam wand for milk foaming. Water for brewing is fed through a thin copper pipe, connected to a cold-water feed that passes through the interior of the steam boiler, heating it as it travels through. The exact length and diameter of the pipe are carefully calculated so that the water reaches the correct temperature when it arrives the group head. In addition to this, the temperature of the group head is stabilized by way of a thermosiphon that continuously runs water from the boiler to the group head then back to the boiler. In this way the large brass and steel mass of the group head maintains temperature consistent with that of the boiler.

One thing a good barista must be mindful of on a heat exchange machine is the tendency of the group head to overheat slightly if left to sit for too long. This can be overcome by a quick flush of (slightly cooler) brew water through the group head, which will cool it down the components to the correct temperature for brewing. Exactly how much water needs flushing through hinges on multiple factors, not least of all the model of machine itself and how long it has been idling for, but 100–150 g/3½–5¼ oz is about right.

The heat exchanger design is epitomized by the E61 group head (see page 89). Now in its sixth decade, it is time-tested and, with a little practice, highly effective in its operation. The E61 has a small lever that is used to commence and end extraction, as well as control pre-infusion.

A double boiler overcomes the conflicting dual-purpose nature of the espresso machine in perhaps the most obvious way – one boiler for brewing coffee and another for steaming milk. The first commercially machine of this kind was the La Marzocco GS. The GS was released in the 1970s, but it's fair to say that double boiler machines didn't really catch on for another 20 years. Most modern commercial espresso machines are now double-boiler models, though, boasting superior levels of temperature control and improved consistency over heat exchanger models.

FINE-TUNING

The obvious next step on from this is a machine that has an individual boiler tank for each group head, allowing for the further refinement and tweaking options. Temperature control on modern machines is done using a PID (proportional-integral-derivative) controller. PID is a generic term for an electronic controller that maintains a set value using control feedback loops. Many common devices use PIDs – cruise control in a car might use one to maintain a certain speed based on calculating incremental changes of the angle of the road over time. In espresso machines, the PID maintains constant water temperature, controllable to the degree, or 1/10 degree in some cases.

Almost all commercial machines have the option of volumetric water control nowadays, allowing buttons to be programmed to dispense a specific volume of water every time they are pushed, but expect to see these replaced with weight sensitive models before too long. Most of the flagship espresso machines now come equipped with pre-infusion timers, but in an ironic turn of events, it's the new wave of paddle-controlled machines that are getting professional baristas most excited; these fully electric machines essentially aim to mimic the pressure profiling options that the modest lever machine offers.

BUYING YOUR OWN ESPRESSO MACHINE

The truth is that making true espresso at home is wasteful, messy, time-consuming and costly. It's far better to go to a café and get someone there to make espresso for you. If you don't have a café nearby, there are two further options. The first is to accept that espresso is too much trouble, buy a good grinder and try one or more of the traditional brewing options detailed between pages 114–145.

The second option is to join the dark side and buy a Nespresso machine. These machines are basically pressurized coffee makers that produce espresso-style coffee (using the term loosely) using pods containing ground coffee. Buying a Nespresso machine means leaving nearly all of your decision-making abilities at the door. The choice of 'espresso blends' are pre-ground, packaged and assigned a suitably nauseating name, designed to evoke an emotional connection. Nestlé grind their coffee in state-of-the art water-cooled roller-mill grinders that operate in a virtually oxygen-free environment, but it can't beat freshly ground stuff. The good news, however, is that you can now buy empty pods and once you start filling them with your own coffee the dynamic changes entirely, and it might just be you who has the last laugh.

MAKING ESPRESSO

Espresso is a method of percolation through a fine metal filter. What differentiates it from normal gravity percolation is pressure. The espresso machine's ability to force water through a coffee bed at high pressure means that the coffee itself can be ground very fine indeed, yet still allow proper percolation and balanced extraction. So what? Well, this is of great benefit because very fine coffee grounds means a very quick extraction, since the surface area increases at an exponential rate as the coffee grounds get smaller. It gets better, though. High pressure also forces water into the interior cell walls of the coffee grounds, extracting stuff that gravity alone would never manage, such as emulsifying oils and dissolving sugars. The product is a complex and concentrated representation of coffee, with a body and texture that cannot be found in any other type of brewing.

The trick to espresso, as with every other brew method, is good extraction (see pages 69–71). Sounds simple, but the problem we face with espresso is the intensity of the process. Venturing to get the very best out of a coffee in an exceedingly short space of time presents similar issues to that of washing yourself with a firehose in 30 seconds.

Good extraction in espresso means a balanced array of aromatic and taste compounds. I'm talking structured bitterness, crisp acidity and lasting sweetness – the same stuff that we aim for with any type of coffee-brewing method. Although all coffees will give up their goods slightly differently, and you can't beat tasting to check quality, eyeballing the extraction rate can, as a bare minimum, tell you when a shot will definitely taste bad. A double espresso usually weighs around 30–45 g/1–1^1/$_2$ oz and should take 25–35 seconds to manifest in its entirety, based on the needs of the coffee. Where one coffee (and I am about to generalize) – say, a light-roasted Kenyan – may prefer a long, dripping, 30-plus second extraction to overcome acidity, another coffee – like a dark Brazilian – might be better suited to a punchier approach to rein in bitterness.

As a general rule of thumb, it's the acids that extract first. This is why underextracted (faster-flowing) espresso has a sour taste to it. Next up is sweetness, and this is a harder one to gauge, because roasted coffee contains very little in the way of actual sugar. Sweetness is as much a perception as anything, but it's typified by good body, associated aromatics and chewy texture. Finally, it's the bitter flavours that come last – slower dissolving, long compounds that give the cup balance but can easily overpower it in over-extracted shots.

So what of aroma? Aromatic qualities are a large part of what differentiates one espresso for another, but pulling shots with an aim of a specific aromatic profile is nigh on impossible. The aromatics in the cup are not a reflection of the barista's skill, but that of the roaster and coffee grower. What can be altered is the way in which the aromatics are perceived through the tweaking of the taste profile. A barista can dial up the acidity in a shot, for example, which might highlight orange or grapefruit aromatics. The same shot pulled a little tighter may taste more bittersweet, giving the effect of chocolate orange or grapefruit marmalade.

This chapter covers an in-depth look in to the art of brewing espresso. Before jumping in, though, be sure that you have read the sections on water (see pages 68–69), extraction and brew ratio (pages 69–71) and grinding (see pages 76–83), for a basic understanding of coffee brewing.

WATER TEMPERATURE

As with any brew method, water temperature plays a part. If you're just starting out, espresso brew temperature shouldn't be too much of a concern as there are plenty of other factors to contend with already. But brew ratio, coffee roast level, coffee variety and processing all can have an effect on the optimal brew temperature. Not all espresso machines have the function to adjust group-head brewing temperature anyway, but the general rule of thumb is that darker roasts require a lower brew temperature (90–92°C/194–198°F) and lighter roasts a higher brew temperature (93–95°C/199–203°F).

DOSING AND DISTRIBUTING

A dose of ground coffee (ranging anywhere from 14–22 g/^{1}/$_2$–^{3}/$_4$ oz) is placed in the clean filter basket

of the group handle. The exact amount you use will depend on the size of the basket itself, as they vary in capacity, but also the desired size and strength of the drink you are making. You'll know if you've overfilled when the portafilter refuses to lock into the group head. Don't underfill, either, as this leaves too much headspace over the coffee, which can cause the cake to get all mushy, leading to greater inconsistency in flow rate. Be sure to weigh how much coffee you are using, at least to begin with, as this will be used to calculate the brew ratio while the shot is pouring. Note that the grounds may require some degree of redistribution by and at this stage, but it will vary on how the model of grinder drops the grounds in the first place.

TAMPING

Next, the coffee is levelled using a flat tamper. Very fine coffee straight from the grinder is prone to being a bit 'fluffy' so we tamp it to remove air pockets and to pack the grounds into an even cake

ABOVE Tamping is all about tightly packing coffee grounds together for a nice, even extraction.

ABOVE LEFT An espresso dose can be measured easily, by first weighing the empty portafilter and setting the scales to zero.

so that it extracts evenly when the water flows through. If the bed of coffee isn't level, the water will follow the path of least resistance, culminating in both over- and underextraction on opposite sides of the bed during the brewing phase. Compacting with sufficient force to remove air pockets is the second goal. The degree to which you tamp has no effect on the rate of extraction, as an espresso machine will soon be pushing on that same bed of coffee with a pressure of 9 bar/130 psi, which is far more forceful that a human arm.

The tamping stage of espresso is something that has been overemphasized in more recent years, resulting in a kind of gratuitous reverence that it simply doesn't warrant. I suppose the mystique surrounding tamping spawns from the ineffectual feeling that you get when you brew espresso, where much of the process is concealed from view, meaning that those elements that are in plain sight become overemphasized and contrived.

PRE-INFUSION

It's typical at this stage to run a little water through the group head before inserting the portafilter. This ensures that fresh brewing water is pumped through from the boiler and makes for better temperature consistency.

The group handle is then inserted into the group head, which locks into place and clamps a rubber gasket over the edge of the filter basket. The seal is relied upon to maintain the necessary pressure for extraction. From here on, in it is important that pre-infusion and extraction follow quickly, since the coffee is now in close proximity to the shower screen and hot components in the group head. Press the button, pull the lever or flip the paddle!

The first contact between water and coffee is the 'pre-infusion', where a small amount of water is dispensed on the grounds to wet them thoroughly. Some machines pre-infuse automatically using flow restrictors or, on newer machines, infusion chambers; other machines feature manual controls. Pre-infusion normally takes 3–10 seconds and it's an important stage, like a warm-up before a quick sprint, which initiates the extraction process, and is thought to even out any inconsistencies there might be in the density of packing of the coffee in the filter basket. The coffee bed expands as it absorbs this first influx of water, which forces any air space that may have been held out of the system. Making adjustments to the length and pressure of the pre-infusion is a difficult skill to master, but offers superior control of extraction from an espresso blend.

The basic rule of thumb is this: the longer the pre-infusion, the faster the subsequent extraction. For example, a 18 g/^{2}/$_3$ oz dose of finely ground coffee with a long pre-infusion may extract the same weight of liquid in the same time as a 18 g/^{2}/$_3$ oz dose of coarser ground coffee that has no pre-infusion. This can be taken to the extreme by grinding very finely indeed and giving a long (10-second-plus) pre-infusion. Exactly why the long pre-infusion makes

such a huge difference is not totally understood; some people suggest that the fine grounds become trapped in the puck (the puck-shaped mound of espresso grounds left after a shot is pulled), but my best guess would be that the fines become free-flowing, actively mobile, particles in the wet puck basket, free to move around in a capillary-like fashion during the initial period of low pressure. When the proper extraction begins, the fines are in a state of readiness and make for a comparatively quicker extraction since the path has been cleared. For more on fine grinds, see pages 80–81.

Taking it to the absolute extreme, even the pressure of the pre-infusion is thought to affect how the puck blooms and the extraction that follows. It's thought that a sudden high-pressure (9-bar/130 psi) pre-infusion has the affect of thumping fines down to the bottom of the puck into a kind of sandbag that restricts flow for the remainder of the extraction. When a low pressure pre-infusion takes place (1–2 bar/14^1/$_2$–29 psi), the bloom is more gentle and the movement of fines less forceful.

EXTRACTION

The next part is the extraction proper, where the system pressurizes and brewed coffee flows from the spout of the group handle. In these first magical moments, you bear witness to the genesis of a unique scarlet-coloured coffee concentrate being brought into the world, never to be faithfully replicated ever again.

The window of tastiness generally lies between a 25- and 35-second extract, depending on the coffee that you're brewing. In this time we would expect to produce an espresso shot of at least the same weight as the dose of ground coffee that was used (brew ratio of 1:1) and up to three times the weight of the ground coffee used (3:1). For me, I look for a brew ratio (see pages 69–71) of around 1.5:1, or to put it in usable figures: 27 g/1 oz of espresso from an 18 g/^{2}/$_3$ oz dose. Darker roasts tend to use a lower brew ratio than light and tend to carry less body than light ones – a lower brew-ratio helps preserve their modesty.

Always keep in mind that brew ratio is only a function of beverage strength, but that the weight of coffee may slow down or speed up the extraction through resistance. Keeping in line with our understanding of balanced extraction, espresso should, in all scenarios, aim to move 18–22 per cent of the mass of the ground coffee into the cup. If the espresso gushes out quickly, it will taste sour and underextracted. If it drips out too slowly, it may taste bitter and astringent.

A good barista can glean some information from the rate of flow and the shape of flow that emanates from the spout of the machine, telling him or her how fresh the coffee is, as well as how far along and how efficient the extraction is. The pale liquid that appears around halfway through the extraction, known as 'blonding', is deemed by many as the stage in which little positive flavour is left to extract. But some good (and important) stuff is extracted towards the end of the run, and we shouldn't get overly obsessed with the gooey red blobs that feature in the early stages (no matter how beguiling they might be).

When the flow of liquid twists, or seemingly attempts to hang on to the portafilter spout, it's a sign that the surface tension of the liquid is increasing. This only happens when the extract has a lower level of solubles, typically towards the end of the run. If you see an uneven stream from the start, there's a good chance that your coffee will be under-extracted. However, visual clues are at best only a mediocre indicator of flavour. The only way to know for sure is to taste your creations.

The extraction is stopped when the espresso is deemed complete. Some machines will do this automatically by measuring the volume of water that has been pumped through the group head. Next-generation espresso machines feature built-in scales that measure espresso weight, allowing the barista to calculate extraction ratio between beverage weight and ground coffee weight accurately on the fly. Some baristas still prefer to do things manually, believing that every shot presents itself differently and requires a certain degree of reactive nurturing. I remain an advocate of programmable buttons, with a dependable response that is specifically tailored to the needs of the individual coffee, dose and grind.

UNDER PRESSURE

Pressure is not something that most people need to worry about when making espresso. Most machines

ABOVE A bottom-less portafilter reveals a beautiful, if a little surreal, espresso extraction in full flow.

are set to the standard 9-bar/130 psi of force and will merrily go about their way. Some modern espresso machines are tackling pressure head-on, though, with the function to adjust pressure through the course of the brew. This adds another parameter to the espresso process, which for many means yet another concern on an already long list of concerns. But if your caffeine tolerance allows it, tinkering with the pressure profile can help to finely tune an extraction to a level of precision that opens up new realms of deliciousness in the cup.

The pressure of the water that is forced through a coffee bed determines the contact time with the coffee in the filter basket. Very low pressure would mean long contact time, and very high pressure a short contact time, but the exact time of contact is also a function of the dose and grind, too.

Having the ability to ramp the pressure up (or down) near the end of an espresso brew affords the barista increased powers. What this all boils down to depends largely on what you are hoping to get out of the espresso. A larger-volume drink made at lower pressure with a coarser grind could be just as balanced and tasty as a shorter-volume drink at high pressure made using a finer grind. They would be two quite different drinks, mind you.

CREMA

For many people, the tan-coloured foam that sits on top of an espresso is an intrinsic part of the espresso experience. But the reverence that it commands is perhaps equalled by its misinterpretation as a gauge of quality. To understand why that is, we must first get to grips with what *crema* (Italian for 'cream') actually is.

In all brewing methods, water will extract some amount of carbon dioxide from ground coffee, and this is apparent in the bloom that we see in pourover brews (see pages 124–133). A dense mound of *crema* is only possible due to the high-pressure nature of espresso brewing, however, where concentrated carbon dioxide is forcefully extracted from ground coffee beans. The sudden decrease in pressure when the first seething red drops of espresso emerge from the spout causes the dissolved carbon dioxide to inflate into larger bubbles very quickly, expanding the volume of the drink so that the cup appears to fill faster than the rate of flow could physically allow. Bubbles are all well and good, but they would be lost immediately without something to stabilize them; that something is a surfactant (a naturally occurring substance that lowers the surface tension of a liquid) in the form of a group of compounds called melanoidins, which are created as part of the Maillard reactions that took place during roasting (see page 55). Melanoidins crowd around the bubbles of carbon dioxide, increasing the bubbles' surface tension and strengthening them into a fairly stable foam. It's no coincidence that an espresso looks so similar to a pint of Guinness when it settles – the bubbles in the stout are stabilized by melanoidins, too, which are formed during the barley-roasting process.

Leave an espresso to sit for long enough and you will eventually notice that the *crema* begins to dissipate. This is a character trait that is consistent among all foams, where the liquid part of the foam begins to drain away. It's possible that the rate of drainage (or the tenacity of the crema) can be used as a rough indicator of quality in espresso, since properly extracted shots are generally awarded with a longer-lasting *crema*.

1 *Crema* fills the glass during the first half of espresso extractions, as carbon dioxide inflates its proportions.

Indeed, an under-extracted shot of espresso generally features less *crema* and the little *crema* it does have it loses at a faster rate. This is a result of the faster extraction, over a shorter period of time, in which less carbon dioxide is drawn out. Less *crema* is also found on older (stale) coffee, which has much less carbon dioxide to give. It's for this reason that I would always question an espresso featuring very little or no crema at all.

Another thing that *crema* is useful for is gauging the strength of the drink. After all, the liquid part of foam is nothing more than a network of the same coffee that sits below it. It is much paler, of course, because of the way that light refracts through the bubbles, but it is a

2 As the finished espresso begins to settle, the *crema* floats, then begins to drain away into the drink below.

3 After a minute or so the gas has mostly dissipated, depriving the drink of some of its volume in the process.

representation of the drink's colour, and therefore strength, nonetheless.

There has been some suggestion in the past that *crema* acts like a kind of security blanket that prevents the escape of volatile aroma molecules. Studies conducted by Nestlé on this topic found that the opposite is actually true, and that in the first few minutes of an espresso's life, the multitude of bursting bubbles, which make up the orange mass of soft *crema*, actually promote the propulsion of aroma molecules away from the drink. While this might appear like something of a win for the *crema*-lovers out there, we need to ask ourselves whether or not we would prefer our aroma molecules floating around above our drinks, or held back for better enjoyment in the mouth.

In my experience, *crema*, by itself doesn't taste particularly nice, and I'm not alone. Certain factions of the speciality coffee industry have instigated a crema rebellion (or as I like to call it, *crembellion*) that has seen some extremists take to spooning off their *crema* before drinking their espresso. I find this kind of thing to be a little severe, however; in clinical trials, *crema* has been found to improve the perceived 'smoothness' of an espresso in both its appearance and the benefits to mouthfeel that it offer. I think it's vital that we view *crema* as more than just a taste contributor, and as a player in the broader multisensory appeal of espresso.

ESPRESSO AND MILK: A MATCH MADE IN HEAVEN

07

INTRODUCTION

A shot of espresso on its own is not to everyone's taste. It's a potent little package of flavour that can sometimes benefit from the tempering effect of milk. Espresso and milk are a great match, too – the fruit, caramel and chocolate qualities of the shot play nicely with the wholesome dairy flavours of the milk, lengthening out toffee, chocolate and dried fruit into an indulgent sipping beverage. For many people, the combination of espresso and milk makes a satisfying substitute breakfast, supplying morning calories as well as essential minerals.

The range of espresso and milk marriages is a wide one, from a splash of espresso in a milkshake through to a blob of milk foam or a coating of milk inside a glass to take the edge off a naked shot. Many of the coffee drinks served in cafés today contain far more milk than coffee. Indeed, some coffee-shop chains have become exceptionally good at masking the flavour of their coffee with, quite frankly, disturbing quantities of milk and additional, usually sweetened, flavourings. But even in the best cafés milk plays a big part in the quality of a cup, both as a delicate and nuanced ingredient and as a medium for controlling the temperature of the drink.

Espresso is not the beginning and end of it all, however. It might surprise you to know that we've been mixing coffee and milk for around 300 years. In this section I will describe how these drinks came into existence, why there is such a powerful affinity between the coffee bean and the cow, and how to produce some of the world's favourite espresso-and-milk drinks.

HISTORY

Coffee and milk or cream have long been seen as natural companions. It was early in the 18th century that the practice of combining them began, but, rather than being enjoyed for its own sake, the drink was regarded at the time as the preserve of children, the elderly and the sick. Mixing milk with tea was established around the same period and for similar reasons. Feeling under the weather? Put some milk in your coffee. Adding cream to coffee was the next step towards creating a more indulgent drink.

In 1727 an English historian, named James Douglas, wrote that many people had an aversion to the intensely bitter taste of black coffee, preferring to have 'mix'd it with either sugar or milk'. Tristram Shandy, the hero of Laurence Sterne's eponymous comic novel published in the 1760s, notably drinks 'two dishes of milk coffee', remarking that the beverage 'is excellently good for a consumption, but you must boil the milk and coffee together – otherwise 'tis only coffee and milk'.

To my mind, boiled milk is rarely tasty and, despite these questionable early attempts to invent the latte, the harmonious pairing of coffee and milk didn't truly occur until the espresso machine was well established in the mid-20th century.

Milk became the companion of the espresso machine for three very good reasons. Firstly, there is the advantage of being able to do two tasks – hydration and caffeination – at the same time. Warm milk can be mixed with hot espresso to create a beverage that slips down easily and provides a pretty good breakfast-in-a-mug for those in a hurry. Next, there is the fact that milk reduces the temperature of the drink slightly, especially in the case of latte served in the traditional Italian way, meaning that the drink can be quaffed with little risk of burning your mouth. Finally, there is the financial angle. Handing over a pocketful of change for 25 ml/1 fl. oz) of something that provides little more than caffeine and flavour can be a little galling. If you lengthen the drink so that it is something to be sipped and savoured, you have a better commercial proposition. Coffee becomes less of an in-and-out, leaning-on-the-bar affair, because the drink takes longer to consume, and the café selling it also has a better chance of selling suitable accompanying foods such as pastries, cakes and doughnuts. Espresso-and-milk drinks benefit everyone.

TYPES OF MILK

Milk is an emulsion consisting of fat globules and a mixture of minerals, proteins, acids, sugars and salts. It is stabilized by the whey protein beta-lactoglobulin, which traps fat globules and suspends them in water. The mixture of fat and water is what makes milk opaque; the emulsion refracts the light and makes the milk look cloudy.

The milk you drink has almost certainly been pasteurized. If it hasn't, you probably live on a farm. Pasteurization kills 99.999 per cent of bacteria, lengthening the shelf life of the product from three days to around three weeks. In the standard pasteurization method, known as HTST (high temperature, short tIme), the milk is rapidly heated above 72°C/162°F for 15 seconds to kill the bacteria. Pasteurization has some disadvantages. It destroys some of the whey proteins in the milk, for example, and reduces mineral content.

'Long-life' or UHT (ultra-high temperature) milk is heated to a whopping 135°C/275°F for two seconds, using jets of blazing-hot steam and vacuums to cool it down. UHT milk has become very popular in Europe (with the UK being a notable exception), but I regard it as vastly inferior to ordinary pasteurized milk.

Some milk is micro-filtered, whereby the cream is separated and pasteurized independently. The whey (watery part) is pumped through tiny apertures that filter out the bacteria spores, and the cream is mixed back in afterwards. This method is slightly less effective at removing harmful bacteria, but more of the milk's natural mineral and protein content is preserved.

Many milk brands are homogenized, too. This process involves firing the milk through very thin pipes, causing the fat molecules to break down and become smaller. The protein in the milk does the job of holding these smaller molecules in place, sustaining the emulsion, and the result is a silky-smooth milk that is not prone to separation, albeit with a slightly blander flavour that its unhomogenized counterpart. I'm not particularly old, but I can still remember having unhomogenized milk delivered in bottles in which the neck had became blocked with the separated cream component.

Whole (full-fat) milk has long been my preference for a cappuccino, latte or flat white. The extra fat in the milk gives the drink a slightly more silky consistency and glossy appearance, which is more than apparent on the palate, and a richer flavour. However, as is normally the case, the tastiest option is often the one condemned as being bad for you. For those concerned about fat content, skimmed

ABOVE Clouds in my coffee, as a turbulent splash of cream drowns in a dark pool of coffee.

and semi-skimmed flavours are available, but I have always considered the loss of quality too great a sacrifice for the sake of a gram or two of dietary fat.

Whole milk contains between 3.25–3.5 per cent fat, while skimmed/skim has about 1 per cent. A typical latte requires about 150 ml/5 fl. oz of milk, meaning that a full-fat latte has about 5 g/$^1/_6$ oz fat and a skimmed latte 1.5 g/$^1/_{18}$ oz – a 3.5 g/$^1/_8$ oz difference per serving. To put it in context, a 150 g/ 5 $^1/_4$ oz bag of nuts has around 70 g/2 $^1/_2$ oz of fat, equivalent to the difference between 20 full-fat and skimmed lattes. Furthermore, new studies have found that the less your milk is tampered with, the better it is for you, regardless of fat content.

Some milk is naturally low in fat. In New Zealand, cows have been selectively bred to produce milk containing 1 per cent fat straight from the udder. Other studies have challenged the conventional belief that fat is bad for us and concluded that the traditionally accepted notion that high-fat diets lead to a greater risk of heart disease may be wrong.

STEAMING MILK

Correctly steamed milk is a fine combination of microscopic air bubbles and warm liquid with a sweet flavour and a light texture. Overheating or scorching milk is a depressingly frequent occurrence in large café chains; it can be identified by a burned taste in the coffee and, rather fittingly, plenty of screaming and rumbling noises emanating from the pitcher while the milk is being abused. Milk-based espresso drinks are not supposed to be scalding-hot, but there are plenty of stubborn coffee-drinkers – in the UK, in particular – who insist on their milk being at a magma-esque temperature, with no care for the resulting loss of flavour. The temperature of milk drinks is not simply about the perception of heat on the palate; it is both a creative and destructive force that must be monitored to maximize natural sweetness in the finished drink. Getting the right temperature is simply a case of not overheating the milk (70°C/158°F and above is bad news), serving the drink in a warm cup and drinking it quickly.

FOAM

In normal conditions, water and air don't mix well. They need a surfactant to bind them together. When you whip cream with a whisk, the fat in the cream acts as a surfactant, a middleman between tiny air bubbles and the water that makes up the rest of the cream. As air is introduced through whipping, the fat in the cream stretches and the cream thickens; it becomes harder for the water in the cream to drain away because the mixture becomes much lighter.

Milk foam is held (for a time) by protein, not fat, in much the same way as egg white holds a meringue in shape. As the milk is heated, its spring-shaped proteins begin to unravel and denature.

There is barely enough protein in milk to sustain the foam and, compared to cream and egg white, milk foam is thin and watery. This makes it highly susceptible to drainage. Drainage involves the foam becoming lighter, until it is eventually only a super-light cobweb-type structure floating on the surface of the liquid. This process begins as soon as you finish steaming milk; it explains why, after being left to rest for a few minutes, a formerly creamy and consistent cappuccino starts to separate, leaving a light, foamy head on top and milky coffee underneath. For many of us, the 'froth-layered-on-top' cappuccino is the definitive cappuccino. But I can promise you that sipping a perfectly aerated cappuccino, which has not yet had time to 'split', will avoid the embarrassing white moustache and bring far more pleasure to your tasting apparatus.

As previously mentioned, drainage is less of a problem with thicker liquids, which is why full-fat milk holds a better foam than skimmed. On the other hand, skimmed milk is easier to foam to begin with, since it contains less fat, which inhibits stability in protein foams.

HOW TO STEAM MILK

Always keep milk in the fridge. Obviously it stays fresher for longer when chilled, but starting with cold milk makes foaming much easier, simply because it gives you more time to 'stretch' or aerate the milk before it reaches the target temperature.

Use a clean pitcher. The exact shape and size of your pitcher is a matter of personal preference (and how many friends you have, of course), but thicker pitchers heat more slowly since the metal absorbs more of the heat. Use a clip-on temperature probe to monitor how much heat is going into the pitcher. Simple 'analogue' thermometers are fine, but I prefer to use an infrared probe because it reacts quickly and offers a digital readout. After plenty of practice, you will no longer need a probe to monitor heat; it can be done by listening and feeling alone (eyes aren't much use here).

The intense swirling and stretching of the milk, as well as the controlled introduction of air, generates enough force to dissolve tiny air bubbles into the milk that will stay suspended for a short time. Properly aerated milk is often referred to as 'micro-foam', since the bubbles have been so closely integrated into the milk that they cannot be seen with the naked eye. Visually the milk will simply appear thicker and creamier. Try to avoid reheating milk; the proteins present in the milk don't work as well the second time around, plus the flavour is not as good.

The following steps explain how to stretch (aerate) a pitcher of milk using the steam wand attachment of an espresso machine, and how to heat it to the desired temperature.

1 Pour milk into the pitcher, so that it is more than half full. Remember that reheating is not advisable, so don't put in more than you need to begin with.

2 Purge the steam wand on the espresso machine to remove any condensation.

3 Place the tip of the steam wand just under the surface of the milk and turn it on at full power. Reduce the power slightly if you're heating a very small volume of milk.

4 Begin stretching the milk out by directing the flow of steam along the circumference of the pitcher, creating a whirlpool of milk. (**A**)

5 To introduce more air, bring the tip of the steam wand right up to the surface, listening for a sharp 'crack' accompanied by a sucking noise. There shouldn't be any large bubbles visible.

6 Continue spinning the milk and stretching it out until you reach 40°C/104°F. At this point, it is harder to stretch the milk because free-flowing fats become a problem.

7 Dip the steam wand further into the milk and keep spinning until you reach 65°C/149°F. (**B**)

8 Immediately turn off the wand.

9 Give the pitcher a light tap to burst any surface bubbles.

10 Swirl the milk froth in quick, tight circles to combine fully. Pour immediately.

THE LATTE

Ordering a 'latte' in an Italian café is likely to result in the arrival of a glass of milk. The word means 'milk' in Italian so if you want a coffee, be sure to place a 'caffè' in front of it. In simple terms, a latte is an espresso topped up with hot milk. It is designed to provide a coffee kick to those who would prefer a less ferocious coffee flavour.

A latte generally comes in a larger cup or glass than a cappuccino would and has slightly less foam. In many mainstream cafés, the caffè latte is a very milky drink indeed – but, given the inflated proportions of the cappuccino in those same establishments, it has become difficult to pinpoint the difference between the two.

I am convinced that most habitual latte-drinkers would happily drink a cappuccino, and vice versa. In spite of the tens of thousands of coffees that I have prepared over the years, I have never met anyone who has protested that their latte was too much like a cappuccino or their cappuccino too much like a latte.

The point is that coffee terminology is far from exact and people who order one of these drinks expect to be served something slightly foamy, not too strong and warm enough to sip but not gulp.

Prufrock Coffee on Shoreditch High Street in London was the first café that I encountered that confronted this lack of discrimination by simply offering its milk-based (double) espresso in three volumetric sizes: 4 oz, 6 oz and 8 oz. In doing so, it identified an obvious truth that had previously escaped us. All latte-drinkers and all cappuccino drinkers want the same amount of coffee and all want textured milk; it's the quantity of milk used to dilute the espresso that differentiates us.

I recommend that a latte is served in a larger cup, with a capacity of 180–200 ml/6-7 fl. oz). I think it's best with a single shot of espresso (18–22 g/^{2}/$_3$-^{3}/$_4$ oz), and topped up with only lightly aerated milk.

LATTE ART

Latte art has been possibly the greatest growth driver for speciality coffee in the past ten years. It wasn't the flavour of great coffee that first got me obsessed with espresso; it was a fascination with pouring latte art – and I know that I'm not alone.

Latte art is not exclusive to the latte. The techniques can be used to decorate any espresso drink containing steamed milk. I should make it clear that I am referring to pouring milk from a pitcher to create a pattern on top of the drink, not pouring milk into the drink then decorating it using a cocktail stick and drops of chocolate sauce. (As impressive as some examples of this might be, it is not a practical way of preparing and consuming coffee.)

Learning how to pour latte art is like learning to pole vault – seemingly impossible until you've done it once. As I describe how latte art works, I hope that you will start to understand why some techniques are successful and others fail.

Freshly steamed milk should be a homogenous mixture of air and milk. It should look like white, glossy paint, without any visible bubbles. The tendency for steamed milk is always for the lighter stuff to rise to the top of the pitcher and the heavier (more viscous) milk to sink to the bottom. Repeated swirling of the pitcher should combat this. It is important that the consistency of the milk remains slick and creamy while you are pouring.

HOW TO POUR LATTE ART

Firstly, the espresso should be freshly pulled (**A**). If left too long the *crema* can begin to drain, making it fluffy and dry. You don't actually need a *crema* to pour latte art, but a good malleable *crema* will enhance your creations with a marbled effect.

A steady pour is the first skill to master. Pour too slowly and the lip of the jug may hold back the foamier milk, allowing only the denser milk to slip away from underneath. Pour too quickly and you give yourself little time to create the art itself, as well as running the risk of splashing the espresso and 'muddying' the *crema*. The jug should be tilted so that you can pour just the right quantity of foamed milk as a unified mass. An over-full pitcher or one that's too small will cause problems.

The initial pour must come from a height (**B**). Steamed milk has a propensity to float on the surface of the espresso. Good latte art takes advantage of this fact, but only in the later stages of the pour. The first stream of milk will punch into the surface of the coffee, sinking into the base of the cup with turbulent

force. At any point after the initial pour, the actual artwork can begin (**C**). To do this, the milk pitcher must be tipped forward slightly to open the width of the lip. (Sometimes it is easier to angle the cup towards the lip of the pitcher slightly.) The jug must also be lowered closer to the surface of the drink, an action that is helped by the tipping of the cup (**D**). When the milk is poured lower, it hits the coffee with less force, causing the light-textured milk to float to the surface and providing white definition against the brown espresso.

Move the milk pitcher steadily and gracefully from side to side (**E**), creating smooth, wave-like patterns on the surface of the drink. The frequency and length of your movements, plus the rate of flow of the milk, will determine the final pattern. Just before the cup is full, raise the pitcher higher so that the milk punches back through the surface, drawing a line through the pattern to bring all the pieces together (**F**).

A

B

C

D

E

F

THE CAPPUCCINO

The modern-day cappuccino is strongly associated with Italian espresso culture, but the cappuccino – in name, at least – is based on a drink that predates the espresso machine by at least 50 years. It has its roots in the *kapuziner*, a popular drink in 19th-century Vienna, which consisted of coffee with a dollop of whipped cream stirred through it. It is commonly believed that the *kapuziner* got its name because it was a similar colour to the brown vestments worn by the holy men of Salzburg's Kapuziner Abbey. This is partly true, but in a more indirect way than most of us probably imagine, since both *kapuziner* and its French equivalent, *capuchin*, were also used at the time to describe colours. When the contemporary cappuccino was invented, it adopted the same name because it was visually quite similar.

The earliest references to the cappuccino as a foamed-milk, espresso-based drink date from the 1950s, not long after the invention of 'true' espresso. By that time, it had become popular in London. 'We really have a beano [party] on a cup of cappuccino,' wrote a columnist for *Punch* magazine in 1957.

Recipes of the era describe the drink as 'an espresso mixed with equal amounts of milk and foam'. This statement is ambiguous. Does it mean a drink of equal parts espresso, milk and foam? Or does it mean an espresso mixed with an indeterminate quantity of equal parts of milk and foam? The two drinks could be quite different.

Most baristas are taught the rule of thirds (the former of the two possible definitions) and many coffee wall charts depict the cappuccino as three equal parts (1:1:1).

Ignoring the fact that a drink made from individual components of espresso, hot milk and fluffy foam is entirely wrong, both visually and texturally, a drink prepared from equal volumes of all three components would probably have been much smaller and much stronger than the drink we think of today as a cappuccino.

Even if all cappuccinos were made using a double espresso, we would only be pouring a mere 60–80 g (60–80 ml/2–3 fl. oz) of combined milk and foam, which comes much closer to the ratio used to make a macchiato (see page 111). I suggest that a more realistic ratio for a cappuccino is 1:2:2 or, indeed, 1:4, where the '4' is a homogenous mixture of milk and air.

As with most members of the Italian espresso and milk family, these drinks tend to be more of a concept that can be customized rather than a strictly defined recipe. But if there is such a thing as a traditional cappuccino, the ratio is more likely to be a single shot of espresso (18–22 g/²/₃–³/₄ oz), topped up with around 100–120 g (100–120 ml/3¹/₂–4 fl. oz) of moderately aerated milk.

THE FLAT WHITE

The flat white has shot to stardom in the past few years, to the point where it is now as commonplace in the world's best cafés as kale salads and Apple laptops. It is hard to believe that a mere ten years ago it was the preserve of only the craftiest of coffee shops – as well as the whole of Australia and New Zealand. Since then, Antipodean espresso culture has successfully exported itself around the world, and the flat white, sporting its signature rosetta leaf, is the poster boy for the revolution.

The history of the flat white in Auckland dates back to the early 1980s, to the original Auckland coffee shop, DKD Café. This late-night bohemian hangout, located in a back room of the Civic Theatre, was famous for its hot chocolate (served with a chocolate fish on the side), but it also served a flat white – basically a black coffee with milk.

I find this intriguing, since I worked in a New Zealand-inspired café in 2000 that had both a 'flat' and a 'flat white' on its menu. The first was a black coffee and the second was a black coffee with milk. I can remember an Australian co-worker explaining to me that the drink we were serving was not a flat white as he understood it and, to emphasize his point, he promptly produced what I can only describe as a small latte.

Early appearances in Australia depict a much milkier drink than you might expect to receive from a café today, placing the drink very close to the latte in its make-up. Some people might argue that the early flat white was in fact a latte in all but name, and it is almost certain that the name was born out of a culture of simple and honest Antipodean ordering, where a 'short black' is an espresso and a 'long black' an americano. It makes perfect sense, therefore, that a white coffee with no foam on top becomes a 'flat white'.

One thing that nearly everyone agrees upon is that the milk in a flat white is textured but not foamy – and this, perhaps, is the major distinction between the flat white and the cappuccino. We must remember that the cappuccino of the 1980s consisted more often than not of espresso and milk with a liberal amount of milk foam spooned on top.

As to the international fame that the 'flattie' is now enjoying, a large chunk of kudos must go to the Flat White café on Berwick Street in London's Soho district. Flat White opened in 2005 and, in doing so, doubled the number of speciality coffee shops in London at the time (Monmouth in Borough Market was the other one). With its simple menu and professional service, Flat White was, and still is, the epitome of laid-back Aussie charm. It has brought the concept of the flat white to the masses and gone on to inspire a generation of coffee-shop operators.

In 2010 the UK's Costa Coffee chain, which accounted for around 1,000 stores at the time, announced that it would be adding the flat white to its menu, describing the drink as 'richer than a latte, creamier than a cappuccino'.

So what exactly is a flat white today? Perhaps the best way to describe the flat white that I make is 'a small latte where some of the milk has been replaced by an extra shot of espresso'. Practically speaking, this means we're looking at around 35–45 g/1 1/4–1 1/2 oz espresso (a double shot) topped up with 120 g (120 ml/4 fl. oz) of lightly foamed milk.

THE MACCHIATO

The macchiato is an excellent drink for those in need of a quick, sharp espresso hit while wishing to avoid the feral potency of a naked shot. A tiny splash of milk in an espresso reins in the temperature of the drink and the addition of a small amount of fat and sugar pulls out caramel, chocolate, vanilla and nutty flavours from the coffee; meanwhile, the body and concentration that we demand from a drink of this size are preserved.

I've served a macchiato to the British prime minister more than once, which makes me think that, if it's good enough for someone running a country, it must be good enough for you and me.

The macchiato is another 'milked' espresso drink whose exact nature is the subject of debate. One consequence of the uncertainty has been a drink served with only the tiniest dollop of milk foam on top when it should contain a larger splash. This inconsistency of approach derives partly from the definition of the word 'macchiato', which in Italian means 'marked'. If you take the translation literally, a dollop of foam on top (to mark the espresso) should suffice, but when it comes to taste this kind of macchiato is hard to tell apart from an espresso.

Surely there must be more to it than a simple blemish of milk? In Italy, the 'mark' of the macchiato is used to describe an espresso that has had a splash of milk added but, owing to the fact that the milk falls through the cream, would otherwise remain indistinguishable from a regular espresso.

A true macchiato should incorporate a targeted splash of steamed milk. I prefer a macchiato that consists of half espresso and half milk, but the beauty of this drink is that it can be tailored to your preference. Top up a 35–45 g/1 ¼–1 ½ oz espresso (a double shot) with 45 g (45 ml/1 ½ fl. oz) of lightly steamed milk. Latte art (see pages 104–106) is entirely possible on a macchiato, but can prove tricky in what is typically such a small cup.

OTHER
BREWING
METHODS

08

INTRODUCTION

For as long as coffee has been consumed, we have been developing new ways to prepare it. As we have seen in Chapter 1, coffee drinkers are historically an enterprising bunch, but it's not just a caffeine-fuelled passion to innovate that has spawned new inventions in the coffee world, it's also an attempt to address a fundamental problem with coffee itself – the fact that it floats when you add water to it. The significance of this fact should not be underestimated. If we to lived in a universe where coffee simply sank, this book would contain considerably fewer pages!

Tea, by contrast, always sinks. It's for this reason that teapots are generally simple, stout and stocky affairs, with their spouts emerging from halfway up, or near the top of the pot. Functionally, a teapot need not be any more complicated than this, since the vast majority of the tea will remain in the pot once the leaves are saturated. Tea leaves are also fairly large compared with coffee grounds, so a simple tea strainer is all that is needed to stop stray leaves.

Coffee ebbs, wanes, swirls and floats. An innocuous knock of a settled coffee pot results in a tumultuous explosion of muddy clouds. If left to settle long enough, the larger grounds will float to the top of the pot and the finer grounds will sink to the bottom. It is, undeniably, a huge inconvenience. So how do we get around this?

Brewers typically fall into one of two camps (though some of the ones listed below could be categorized as both): immersion brewers and percolation brewers. Immersion brewers, like a French press, give sustained contact between coffee and water, offering a fair amount of control to the operator. Percolation brewers are slightly different, because they work by allowing coffee to flow through a bed of grounds, extracting flavour as it goes. It's kind of like the difference between having a bath and having a shower. One routine gives a thorough soak, while the other is more of a complete rinse.

The type of brewer and the method used for brewing determines the style of coffee you get in the cup: for example, a French press typically results in a full-bodied cup with a rich mouthfeel, while paper-filtered coffee is usually more delicate. An understanding that the positive characteristics of the bean can be highlighted through the method of preparation will often lead to delicious coffee.

Be sure to read about brew temperature on page 69 and grinding in Chapter 5 before diving into these brewing methods. I would also recommend purchasing a pour-over kettle (with its distinctive long spout) to help distribute water evenly and accurately for the cloth filter (see pages 126-7) and paper filter (see pages 128–9) methods.

LEFT A beautiful syphon brewer uses vapour pressure to mix water and coffee, and then to un-mix them! (see pages 138–141)

OPPOSITE Each brewer produces a unique style of drink that can and should be tailored to the needs to the individual coffee. From full-bodied immersion brewing, to light and delicate pour-over coffee, I encourage you to explore them all.

THE POT

Short of placing ground coffee in a bowl with hot water and drinking it (see pages 72–73), the coffee pot is the simplest coffee brewer out there and the only one which foregoes filtration altogether.

Early references to coffee brewing in Constantinople refer to a copper *ibrik*, in which 'powder' is mixed with water once it 'boyls', then, once brewed, is 'snatched quickly from the fire' and poured into cups, leaving most of the grounds in the pot. An *ibrik* is a wide-bottomed pot with a spout near the top and a straight handle usually at right angles to the pot. This Turkish design was copied and improved once it arrived in Europe, and new iterations continued to appear in the 17th and 18th centuries.

A classic coffee pot is usually tall, with a spout emanating from the middle or near the bottom – a design element that aims to restrict the migration of grounds from the top and bottom of the pot into the cup. The taller the better, since lanky pots further increase the distance between the spout and the extremities of the pot.

Pot-brewed coffee is not without its problems, though; grounds always find a way out and as the pot empties, the problem is compounded. Once the technology existed, the Turks got around this issue by simply grinding as finely as possible. Most of the coffee then sinks to the bottom as intended, but it easily swims through the spout when the pot is disturbed, resulting in a thick, muddy and over-extracted cup that evidently, in the Turkish manner, requires sugar and flavourings to become palatable.

This recipe follows the traditional Turkish custom for brewing coffee and will make enough for two cups. It's not going to be the greatest cup of your life, but it does make an interesting coffee drink, while breaking a few rules along the way.

HOW TO BREW TURKISH COFFEE

1 Grind 30 g/1 oz coffee and place it in a pot, or ibrik. Add sugar to taste – around 15 g/½ oz should be fine.

2 Add 400 g (400 ml/13 ½ fl. oz) cold water and then 2 g/¹⁄₁₆ oz ground cardamom, if desired.

3 Stir everything until the sugar has dissolved. Heat the pot on a stove until the contents boil. The mixture will froth up at this point, so quickly remove it from the stove and give a quick stir.

4 Place the pot back on the stove and repeat step 3.

5 Boil for a third time, remove from the heat, but don't stir. Pour the coffee into Turkish cups. Wait a few minutes before drinking.

LEFT The traditional Turkish ibrik is one of the oldest coffee brewers, but it's sadly lacking in the technical department.

THE MOKA POT

The moka or stove-top pot is often incorrectly identified as an espresso maker – it's not, of course – only espresso machines make espresso. Another common misapprehension is that the moka pot always boils the brewing water, causing it to overextract the coffee, which results in a bitter cup. That being said, for many of us the moka pot will always be associated with over-extracted, black, sooty cups of coffee, masquerading as espresso.

While I cannot deny that I have been served terrible drinks from moka pots, I must qualify that statement with the fact that the coffee produced in a moka pot can be excellent if the all the rules are adhered to. Come to think of it, the moka pot might be the single most misunderstood piece of coffee-related paraphernalia out there. Those who love, cherish and use one regularly are generally not using them correctly, and those who scorn them do so because they have only ever even served bad coffee from one.

HISTORY

The moka pot was first patented by Alfonso Bialetti in 1933 and sold under the name 'Moka Express', but didn't become popular until after World War II. Constructed from aluminium, and featuring an iconic design, they warmed up quickly and became a low-cost and convenient option for the home user.

The inner workings of the moka pot function according to the same principles as the pumping percolator, a forerunner to the syphon coffee maker and the grandfather of pressure-operated coffee brewers. In the pumping percolator, water is heated and then pushed from the base of the pot by steam pressure into a second compartment in the top of the pot, which contains the coffee and a filter. The water then percolates down (like any other filter system) into a third section in the middle of the pot, and can then be poured out through a spout. If it sounds complicated

it's because it is, but the pumping percolator was an almost completely autonomous coffee maker – not bad considering it first appeared around 1820.

The moka pot is slightly different, in that it percolates up, by way of an inverted funnel that is submerged in water at the beginning of the process. Steam pressure builds in the headspace of the lower part, forcing the water through the funnel, up through the coffee bed, then out through the pipe in the top chamber. The first machine to brew coffee like this was invented in 1833 by an Englishman called Samuel Parker. However, it was Bialetti's Moka Express that made this kind of brewer popular. In just over ten years the 'Express' sold 20 million units. It became the go-to brewer for home use.

USING A MOKA POT

Let's get one thing straight from the start: if used correctly, a moka pot can make excellent coffee. There are a few considerations beyond the normal range that must be factored in, however.

Moka pots come in a vast range of sizes, some of which are comically large, and others that are absurdly small. Beware of bigger pots, because unless you have a very big heat source to match it, they can take a long time to brew and are highly susceptible to overextraction. This is one of the major flaws in the moka pot: the bigger the pot, the longer the brew time, meaning that grind size must be increased for larger pots to avoid astringent and dull flavours from overextraction. Some moka pots overcome this by including a weighted valve that prevents the water from percolating up until the necessary pressure is achieved – it's important to know whether your pot has this for the brewing process to be effective (see the following page).

Beyond the normal balancing of brew water to coffee ratio, I would also advise that you brew to the maximum capacity of the pot. This is because the less water you put in, the more headspace, and the more headspace, the easier the water is pushed into the top chamber. The quicker the water goes, the lower the temperature it will be, since it has had less time near the heat source.

You're probably getting the picture by now: brewing with a moka pot is quite an art, but very rewarding when it produces great results. Go for medium to dark roasts in this brewer, perhaps a light espresso roast, even.

BREWING COFFEE WITH A MOKA POT

Makes: 2 strong cups (if using a 200 g/7 oz) capacity pot
Brew ratio: 1:5 (200 g/7 oz: 1 litre/1 ³/₄ pints)
Grind: Fine filter

1 For moka pots without a weighted valve, you should first boil your 1 litre/32 fl. oz brewing water in a separate pot. If your moka pot has a weighted valve, pour the cold water directly into the bottom pot. (**A**)

2 Weigh and grind 40 g/1 ½ oz coffee and place it in the filter. (**B**)

3 Fill the base of the top section with 200 g/ (200 ml/6³/₄ fl. oz) hot water and assemble everything together (note that the water level for any pot should never exceed the pressure release valve on the base of the pot). (**C**)

4 Place the moka pot on the stove set over a medium heat. Open the lid and keep an eye on the process, as the water boils and the coffee starts to appear. You can control the rate by lowering the temperature on the stove, which in turn controls extraction.

A

B

C

5 Listen and look out for any bubbling – this indicates that steam is coming through, and at this point, turn the heat off. (**D**)

6 Quickly run cold water over the outside of the pot to halt the brewing process.

7 Serve the coffee and allow to cool a little before tasting. (**E**)

THE FRENCH PRESS

In Europe, the French press, *cafetière*, or plunge pot is probably still the most common method of brewing fresh coffee at home. It functions like any other coffee pot, but with the addition of a plunger that drives a filter down through the brew water, coaxing all but the smallest insoluble grounds to the bottom of the pot. The French press is a fantastic way to brew coffee, since it is a fully immersed brew that retains plenty of body in the coffee and is easy to control. The downside to the French press is the sacrifice of cleanliness and acidity that paper filter brewing does so well.

HISTORY

In 1852, a patent was filed in France for an 'Infusion Coffee Maker' by two Frenchmen, named Mayer and Delforge. The title of the brewer correctly identifies the key feature of this early brewer – infusion. Here was a coffee maker that allowed the user to dictate exactly how long the coffee was steeped for before removing the grounds, and therefore gave greater control over the flavour extraction. This early French press also granted a simple way to infuse and filter coffee in a single pot, without the need for a constant heat source or other paraphernalia.

Unfortunately, the machine was flawed, since the technology at the time made it difficult to manufacture a moving mesh filter that successfully clung to the sides of the pot. Coffee was muddy and the pot difficult to use. The principles were in place, though, and other pots followed, some using complex spring mechanisms and others incorporating a two-stage filtering process to remove finer grounds, not unlike the modern Espro Press. These days, the best press pots are made using nylon filters, which were first introduced in the 1980s, with secure-fitting rubber gaskets.

USING A FRENCH PRESS

The trick with a French press is patience and a gentle touch. The associated 'sludge' that can haunt the bottom of your cup is a sign of poor brewing technique and a result of fine grounds sneaking through the apertures of the filter. Almost all grinders produce fines (see pages 80–81), and there's little that can be done about them other than sifting them out in a tea strainer after brewing. You can, however, limit the sludge by skimming the top, plunging the filter gently and allowing the brew to sit for a few minutes before pouring.

If the sludge is still getting you down, you can always pass the brewed coffee through a paper filter before serving. You'll lose some body from the coffee, of course, but the extraction ratio will remain the same and clarity will also improve.

TIPS WHEN BUYING A FRENCH PRESS

- Look for a French press that features a secure-fitting filter.
- Bear in mind that steel pots will lose heat quickly unless they are double-walled.
- In my opinion, nylon filters are generally better than metal.
- Buy the smallest pot you can get away with.
- Half-filling a large pot is bad practice as the material of the pot draws heat from the brewing water.

BREWING COFFEE WITH A FRENCH PRESS

Makes: 2 cups
Brew ratio: 1:15 (66 g/2 ¼ oz: 1 litre/1 ¾ pints)
Grind: Coarse

1 Preheat your French press with hot water (then pour the water away).

2 Set the French press on a set of digital scales.

3 Grind 22 g/¾ oz coffee and add it to the French press. (**A**)

4 Pour in 330 g (330 ml/11 fl. oz) hot water (**B**), then give it a quick stir. (**C**)

A

B

5 Allow to sit for a further 30 seconds.

6 Skim the orange foam off the top of the brew water with a spoon. (**D**)

7 Place the lid on top and begin gently pressing the plunger (**E**). If you feel too much resistance, slow down and/or stop for a few seconds.

8 Once the plunger is completely depressed, let the brew rest for 5 minutes.

9 Serve, pouring a little into each cup and then topping up – this ensures the even distribution of insoluble particles. Leave a little water in the pot.

C

D

E

FILTER COFFEE

Filters have been around for thousands of years, with even ancient Egyptian tombs depicting water-treatment filters as far back as 1500 BC. The physical filtering of coffee probably didn't exist until the end of the 17th century, after coffee had become readily available in Europe. Not surprisingly, really, filters are technically very clever bits of apparatus, regardless of what shape or form they take. Industrialization helped make the filter more common, meaning that filter coffee didn't truly become a reality for the common man until the turn of the 20th century. Typically the filter is made from steel, nylon, paper or cloth, but there have been many materials used as mediums for coffee filtering in the past, from cloths made out of woven horsehair, to silk, porcelain and hemp.

Depending on where you come from, filter coffee can refer to an assortment of brewing methods – in many parts of Europe it simply means a black coffee, which is fair to an extent, since almost all brewing methods require some kind of filter. In this book, 'filter' is applicable to any type of brewing method where water percolates through coffee placed in/on a semi-permeable barrier using only the power of gravity. That is, no immersion, pump, vacuum or press is involved.

Filter coffee, in general, is a reasonably easy and clean way to brew coffee at home. Coffee prepared in this manner requires a filter to hold the grounds, which itself is often held within another vessel, and a pot to collect the brewed liquid underneath. The weight of the brewing water forces the brewed coffee through a filter, which in turn drips or runs out of the bottom. Producing great results that are repeatable is more difficult than in a French press (see pages 120–123) or Aeropress (see pages 134–137), since it is much harder to control the infusion time. When brewing coffee this way the infusion is regulated by adjusting the speed at which the water is added to the filter, the amount of coffee used, and how fine or coarse the grind is.

A NOTE ON POURING

The way in which coffee grounds are wetted and agitated is of particular importance to filter brewing.

Pouring technique will exert an influence over the brew time, turbulence and brew temperature, all of which affect the extraction of flavour. You may choose to use a pouring kettle, which aids in evenly wetting the coffee during the bloom and the remainder of the brewing steps, and provides a consistent, controllable flow of water.

More water in the filter means a greater weight forcing the brewed coffee through the filter. More water also means a higher brew temperature overall, since it quickly heats up the brewing vessel to near the temperature of the brewing water. A material like aluminium, for example, has a high thermal conductivity and will quickly draw energy heat away from the brew if it isn't preheated. Plastic, on the other hand, is a good insulator of heat and will keep the brew temperature quite stable. Conversely, an excessively slow pour means that your brew may struggle to reach an acceptable temperature (to best extract sweetness), and may loiter around in the filter for too long, potentially becoming bitter or overextracted. For more on brew temperature, see pages 68–70.

Pouring in such a way that all the grounds are evenly soaked is crucial, too, and doing this in such a way as to agitate the coffee will improve the flow of liquid around the coffee, causing it to extract faster.

A NOTE ON BLOOMING

Blooming, as the name eloquently suggests, is one of the more delightful sights in coffee brewing. The bloom occurs when fresh coffee is first wetted by a splash of hot water, most commonly in filter brewing. As the ground coffee absorbs the water, carbon dioxide purges out from the bean and carbonates the brew mixture – yes, those bubbles are the same ones as you get in a glass of Coke. The effect is a curiously attractive belching and expansion of the coffee bed, often doubling in size in 10 seconds with very fresh coffee. Besides the visual gratification from witnessing coffee as a living, 'breathing' entity, blooming is actually thought to be an important part of brewing a good cup of coffee, especially in filter brewing.

When carbon dioxide is purged from the

grounds, it forms a tiny barrier of outward force between the brew water and the coffee grounds themselves. The gas is thought to impede the access of water to all the wonderful solubles held within the grounds, so by allowing the bloom to expand and subside a little, we are essentially displacing the carbon dioxide before adding the bulk of the brewing water. In immersion brewing, it is questionable whether blooming the coffee

ABOVE The Chemex coffee brewer has been a cult brewer for over 70 years, and even features in New York's Museum of Modern Art.

actually makes much difference to the cup, as the mixture is usually stirred, but in filter brewing, wetting the grounds for 10–20 seconds is an important step to help with creating an even bed and even extraction of grounds during percolation.

CLOTH-FILTER BREWING

At its best, a cloth filter can produce a wonderful cup of coffee, benefiting from some of the mouthfeel of a French press brew, but without the muddiness that can sometimes haunt a French press. I've chosen to place cloth filters in a separate category to reusable filters, since they have a finite lifespan and they offer a very different style of brew compared to metal and nylon.

HISTORY

The first cloth coffee filters appeared some time around the beginning of the 18th century. They originally comprised either a separate filter attached to the mouth of a coffee pot, which 'caught' the grounds as they exited the apparatus, or a pot that held a muslin filter from its rim, acting like a giant suspended tea bag in some ways. The latter is also known as a 'biggin' – possibly a corruption of 'bag-in', or from the Dutch word *beggelin*, meaning to 'filter down'. Biggin pots with cloth filters are now becoming rare finds in antiques' markets, but there are plenty of the more modern enamel versions still knocking around.

USING A CLOTH FILTER

One of the main benefits of cloth filter over paper is that cloth allows the passing of flavourful coffee oils into the cup. The downside of the cloth filter is that fine grounds easily clog it up, so they can be difficult to clean and maintain. Once a cloth filter clogs up, bad things happen. The clogged cloth restricts the passing of coffee through the filter; in the worst case, this can completely stall the filtering process altogether, leaving the brew to overextract. Also, if the grind is too coarse, the water will pass through very quickly, so as always the degree of grind is very important here.

On a recent trip to Japan, I was introduced to a barista at Bar Tram in Tokyo who brewed exclusively using cloth filters. True to Japanese form, he had spent years training under a master who taught him how to craft his own filters from a unique grade of fabric and some bent wire. The ritual of using the thing was no less intense and observant, using a finer grind of coffee than the norm (roasted on a tiny countertop copper drum) and poured very slowly over the course of 2–3 minutes. I was honoured when he gave me one of his filters to take away and the step by step images go some way towards recognizing this approach to cloth brewing.

You can have a go at making your own filter, of course, or buy one like the Woodneck brewer made by the Japanese brand Hario. The Superbags brand of micron filters is also a very good solution. Intended for clarifying stocks in the kitchen, micron filters are highly durable, plus they can be purchased in either 100- or 250-micron varieties, giving you a

A

little more control over what gets through. I've found Superbags' micron filters to be a very effective means of brewing lots of coffee all at once. Cloth brews benefit from a finer grind than paper filters, because the water is prone to pass through cloth much quicker; grinding even finer helps slow it down, but as with all gravity brews, this will be contingent on how high you fill the filter and the resulting downward force that is applied by the brewing slush.

CLOTH FILTER BREW 'TOKYO STYLE'

Makes: 1 cup
Brew ratio: 1:12 (83 g/3 oz: 1 litre/1 ¾ pints)
Grind: Fine filter

1 Rinse the cloth filter with plenty of hot water.

2 Place a cup on a set of digital scales.

3 Grind 20 g/¾ oz coffee and add it to the filter (**A**).

4 Reset the scales and pour 50 g (50 ml/1 ¾ fl. oz) water evenly over the grounds and hold the filter over the cup. (**B**)

5 Allow to bloom for 30 seconds.

6 Pour 190 g (190 ml/6 ½ fl. oz) of water evenly and slowly over the grounds in a spiral fashion, working from the outside into the middle then back again, controlling the flow rate by slowing down or speeding up your pouring. (**C**)

7 Allow all of the coffee to drip through, which should take about another 1–2 minutes.

8 Allow to cool for 4–5 minutes, then serve (**D**). While the coffee cools, clean the filter then pop it in a container of water and store it in the refrigerator.

Note: I have used a pour-over kettle (with its distinctive long spout) to help pour the water evenly and accurately.

B

C

D

PAPER-FILTER BREWING

Paper filter brewers are sometimes referred to as 'pour-over' or 'drip' coffee. Paper is a cheap and easy way to make clean and delicious coffee, plus it's easy to travel with or take to work.

There is quite a range of paper filters available today, but they all do much the same thing. Besides the classic ceramic filter holder, you can now get various plastic models, with the Hario V60 being a popular choice among baristas (it also comes in ceramic and glass models). Chemex is another popular paper-filter brewer, and is available in a multitude of sizes to fit your needs. Finally, there is the Clever Brewer, which almost deserves a section to itself. The Clever Brewer looks like any other pour-over cone, the difference being that it has a tap/faucet on the bottom. This means that you can control the infusion time in the same way as a French press and other immersion brewers – a very happy medium.

HISTORY

Paper filters were explored by coffee innovators from the 17th century onwards, with records of patents as far back as the late 1600s that incorporated paper filters into their designs. It's quite likely that these brewers were not completely functional, however, since wood-pulp paper was not invented until 1843, and it's only with the papers that followed that the required level of 'wet strength', porosity, particle retention and flow rate could be achieved.

In 1885, Dr. Heinrich Boehnke-Reich published a book called *Der Kaffee in seinen Beziehungen zum Leben* (*Coffee and its Relationship to Life*), which was significant in that it took a detailed look into coffee preparation methods. Boehnke-Reich correctly pointed out that cloth filters, if not cared for, imparted rancid flavours to brewed coffee. Paper filters were beginning to grow in popularity, and this was partly due to economic reasons. Coffee could be ground finer when using paper so people compensated by using less of it.

It wasn't until 1908 that the true innovation in paper filtering came about. A German housewife called Melitta Bentz invented a one-cup filter device, but with the addition of a paper disc inside. The filter was constructed from aluminium and it flew off the shelves in Germany due to its ease of use and effectiveness. The familiar 'cone' shaped filter was a later innovation that came about in the 1930s.

USING A PAPER FILTER

Filtering through paper, like cloth, works in two ways: volume filtration, where particles are caught on the bulk of the filter, and surface filtration, where particles are trapped on the surface of the filter itself.

One of the best things about filtering with paper is the clarity of the coffee. I've seen Chemex brews that could quite easily be mistaken for fine wines, with their rich mahogany colour and perfect transparency. Brewing with paper is a good way of amplifying the sweetness of a coffee, but it can sometimes misplace the body that might be present in a French press brew. I am personally of the belief that some of the sweetness comes from a mental association with the deep-red hue of a paper brew – it appears to be sweeter and therefore it is.

There are a whole bunch of different filter cones and papers available now and they don't all work in the same way. For example, the Kalita brewer has ribbed sides and a big flat bottom, which tends to slow the brew down. This means you can brew a relatively small amount of coffee without the danger of it gushing through too quickly and underextracting. The famed Hario V60, which has become the staple of coffee bars the world over, has a pointed cone-shaped paper and a wide aperture at the base of the cone. This makes for a faster brew, so you have to compensate by either using more coffee (and brewing more coffee) or grinding finer, to improve resistance in the coffee bed and speed up extraction.

BREWING WITH A PAPER FILTER

Makes: 3 cups
Brew ratio: 1:15 (66 g/2 ¼ oz: 1 litre/1 ¾ pints)
Grind: Filter

1 Place your paper filter in its cone or holder on a set of digital scales. (**A**)

2 Rinse the paper filter with plenty of hot water. This stops your coffee from tasting of paper. (**B**)

3 Grind 32 g/1 oz coffee and add it to the filter. (**C**)

D

4 Reset the electronic scales and pour 50 g (50 ml/1 ³/₄ fl. oz) of hot water evenly over the grounds. (**D**)

5 Allow to bloom for 30 seconds, then give it a quick stir. (**E**)

6 Pour 430 g (430 ml/16 fl. oz) of hot water evenly and slowly over the grounds in a spiral fashion (to ensure that the grounds are evenly wetted) until the paper is three-quarters full, then maintain the same speed of pouring to keep the water at that level until there's nothing left in your jug/pitcher. (**F**)

7 Allow all of the coffee to drip through the filter, which should take about another 2–3 minutes.

8 Finally, remove the filter, allow to cool for 4–5 minutes, then serve. (**G**)

E

F

G

REUSABLE FILTERS

These days we do most of our filtering with disposable paper filters (see pages 128–131), because it's clean, cost-effective and makes nice coffee. Go back 200 years however, and paper filters were not so easy to come by. A repeatable, clean process was required to make consistent coffee; the cloth filter (see pages 126–7) was one solution, and the other was metal. Metal is a convenient option since it produces no waste, and also, unlike paper and cloth, it imparts absolutely no flavour in to the coffee.

One of the first examples of a metal filter originated in France and was called the De Belloy filter pot. Sadly, little is known about this pot, but it was essentially a pot with a perforated insert that held the grounds and allowed the passing of brewed coffee.

It wasn't until the German Ardnt'sche filter, of 1887, that a woven metal mesh was used – for which it won a gold medal at the 1900 World Exhibition in Paris. It looked like a camping mug with a lid and a hole at the bottom, covered by a flat metal mesh filter.

The problem with metal and nylon filters is that the aperture of the filter is usually insufficiently small, which itself presents two distinct issues. The first issue is resistance. The more coarse the filter the less physical stopping power it provides, meaning that brew water will quickly wash through, and the coffee will be under-extracted. Under-extraction can be overcome by grinding finer, but the second problem is that of fines passing through. Quite simply, a coffee particle that is smaller than the holes in the filter will end up in the cup. At best this will make a sludgy cup and at worst the coffee will have a gritty mouthfeel. In my experience, the only neat solution to both problems is to make a lot of coffee – hey, it could be worse. Increasing the volume of grounds in the filter slows down the percolation of water and means you don't have to grind the coffee too finely.

BREWING USING A METAL OR NYLON FILTER

Makes: 6 cups
Brew ratio: 1:15 (66 g/2 ¼ oz: 1 litre/1 ¾ pints)
Grind: Filter

1 Grind 66 g/2 ¼ oz coffee and place it in the filter.

2 Put both the collecting vessel and filter on a set of digital scales. You will need 1 kg (1 litre/1 ¾ pints) of hot water in total.

3 Reset the scales and pour 100 g (100 ml/3 ½ fl. oz) of hot water evenly over the grounds. Allow to bloom for 30 seconds, then give a quick stir.

4 Continue to pour the remaining water evenly and slowly over the grounds in a spiral fashion, working from the outside into the middle, so that the grounds are evenly wetted. Continue to pour in a spiral fashion until the filter is three-quarters full, then maintain the same speed to keep the filter at that level until you've used all of the hot water.

5 Allow all of the coffee to drip through – it should take about 2–3 minutes. Remove the filter and let the coffee settle for 5 minutes before pouring.

LEFT A Vietnamese metal filter: less effective than paper or cloth, but better than a sieve/strainer!

THE CLEVER DRIPPER

The Clever dripper is just as clever as its name suggests. While it may look like any other plastic filter cone, this dripper has the distinct advantage of a valve on the base that controls when the coffee is allowed to drip out of the bottom of the brewer. This gives you the best of both worlds – the clean style of cup associated with a paper filter, but the full-immersion brewing control of a French press or Aeropress. It wont make up for the loss of body that paper removes from the brew, but the Clever dripper does allow you to grind a little coarser and brew for a little longer, affording you slightly more greater control over what goes in to the cup.

The Clever dripper is made out of plastic and comes with a lid, which means your brew water stays well insulated during the steep time. The valve opens once the brewer is placed on the cup of carafe, but remains shut when the dripper is sat on a flat surface. The Clever dripper uses standard ³/₄ cup percolator paper filters with flat bottoms.

Unlike normal pour over brewing, I see no reason to bother with the blooming stage, since the filter will be filled with water, stirred, and the coffee immersed for a good length of time. With regular gravity-filtering the bloom is essential to prevent the initial input of water trickling through too quickly and under extracting.

How you brew with this device is really up to you. You can follow a classic paper filter recipe and allow the coffee to drip through after a quick steep, or follow a French press recipe and keep the brew immersed for a few minutes. The recipe below sits somewhere in the middle of the two.

BREWING WITH A CLEVER DRIPPER

Makes: 3 cups
Brew ratio: 1:15 (66 g/2 ¼ oz: 1 litre/1 ³/₄ pints)
Grind: Coarse filter

1 Place a paper filter into the cone of the dripper.

2 Rinse the paper with plenty of hot water and open the valve to let it drain away.

ABOVE The Clever dripper lives up to its name by offering the best bits of gravity and immersion brewing.

3 Grind 24 g/³/₄ oz coffee and add it to the filter.

4 Put the dripper on a set of digital scales. Reset the scales and steadily pour 400 g (400 ml/13 ½ fl. oz) hot water evenly over the grounds

5 After 30 seconds, give a quick stir.

6 Allow to brew for 90 seconds then give a quick stir. Sit the dripper on a carafe, automatically opening the valve and allowing the coffee to percolate through.

7 Once the percolation is complete, remove the dripper and allow the coffee to sit for a further 2 minutes before serving

THE AEROPRESS

The Aeropress is something of an accidental phenomenon. It was developed to be a cheap alternative to espresso coffee at home and on the move, but actually turned out to be a completely different kind of brewer, with a versatility and cult following that I'm sure its inventors could never have imagined in their wildest dreams.

The genius of the Aeropress is that it borrows the best bits of other brewing methods: the control of a French press, the cleanness of a paper filter and the innovation of a reversible brewer. Couple that with portability and a low price tag, and you truly have a brewer to be reckoned with! In fact, the Aeropress is perhaps the only brewer that can claim indifference to grind size and brew time. Long, coarse brews work just as well as much finer, shorter brews, and this is thanks to its unique design and operation.

The Aeropress was launched in 2005 by Aerobie, the same company that make the super-fast frisbees. Its unassuming form looks much like a giant syringe, and while not the most aesthetically pleasing brewer out there, its plastic construction has afforded it superior brew control and durability. The only major downside to brewing with an Aeropress is that it only makes enough coffee for one person – but you can't have it all, I suppose.

USING AN AEROPRESS

In an Aeropress, coffee is dropped into the larger plastic cylinders, the brewing chamber, which connects to the filter holder. The cylinder is placed on top of a cup, or similar receptacle. Water is added, stirred, and the brew is timed. When complete the second cylinder is slid in through the top of the first, creating a tight-fitting seal around the rubber gasket. The top is then gently pressed, increasing the pressure inside the larger cylinder, and forcing the brewed coffee through the paper filter. Once all of the liquid has percolated through the coffee bed, the plastic filter holder can be unscrewed and the spent coffee puck is simply popped out, leaving behind a device that is so miraculously clean that you might be tempted just to place it back on the shelf!

Because the Aeropress combines immersion brewing, a paper filter and pressure to extract, you can play around with grind size and brew time to achieve different styles of brewed coffee – anything from a high-extraction espresso style drink (I use the term loosely here), through to something more akin to a French press brew. Another benefit of the Aeropress is that its plastic construction insulates better than glass, meaning that the temperature of the extraction has a better consistency than that of a filter brew, for example. Beware of grinding too finely when using an Aeropress; when pressed, the plunger cylinder creates a pressurized system inside the brewing chamber, but if the filter gets clogged, you will find that all you are achieving is the compression of the air inside the system. At that stage, brute force is your only option.

HOW TO GET MORE OUT OF YOUR AEROPRESS

If you're making coffee for two or more people, there are other better-suited brewers to this purpose, but you can try brewing a strong concentrate and adding water to bring it back to the correct brew strength. Try dropping in 30 g/1 oz* fine filter grind to the brew chamber and pouring over 240 g (240 ml/8 fl. oz) water. Brewed for approximately 40 seconds, it will produce a concentrate that can be mixed with a further 200 g (200 ml/6 3/4 fl. oz) water for a balanced cup.

Note: You can also buy a fine metal filter for the Aeropress, bringing it even more in line with a French press-style brew.

* This is about the most that an Aeropress will take before getting blocked.

THE QUICK FILTER BREW METHOD

Makes: 1 cup
Brew ratio: 1:15 (66 g/2 ¼ oz: 1 litre/1 ¾ pints)
Grind: Filter
This method is much quicker than the inverted long brew (shown on the next few pages). It makes a stronger cup that retains balance and should please those after a slightly more punchy cup.

1 Pop the paper filter in the filter basket and rinse with hot water.

2 Clip the filter basket onto the bottom of the brewing chamber and sit the Aeropress on your mug or jug/pitcher, which in turn should be set on a set of digital scales.

3 Weigh and grind 16 g/½ oz coffee and drop it into the brew chamber.

4 Reset the scales and pour in 240 g (240 ml/ 8 fl. oz.) hot water and stir. Allow to sit for 1 minute.

5 Give it a quick stir, then insert the plunger cylinder. Immediately begin pressing – this should take 20 seconds to complete. Allow to cool slightly (while you clean up), pour and enjoy.

THE INVERTED LONG BREW METHOD

My preferred brewing method with the Aeropress, this has the benefit of a long, controlled steep time associated with the French press. It requires fitting the Aeropress together in a slightly irregular order.
Makes: 1 cup
Brew ratio: 1:15 (66 g/2 ¼ oz: 1 litre/1 ¾ pints)
Grind: Coarse

1 Pop a paper filter in the filter basket and rinse with hot water.

2 Turn the Aeropress upside-down and insert the plunger cylinder about 10 mm/⅓ inch down into the base cylinder so that the gasket is secure. (**A**)

A

B

C

D

E

F

G

3 Place the upside-down brewer on a set of digital scales, so that the water and coffee can be added to the brewing chamber.

4 Weigh and grind 16 g/½ oz coffee and drop it into the brew chamber. (**B**)

5 Reset your scales and pour in 240 g (240 ml/ 8 fl. oz) hot water and stir. (**C**) (**D**)

6 Allow to brew for 3 minutes, then briefly stir again and clip on the filter basket. (**E**)

7 Turn the Aeropress over and gently press all of the liquid out – this should take no more than 20 seconds – into a cup or carafe. (**F**) (**G**)

8 Allow to cool slightly (while you clean up) and enjoy. (**H**)

VACUUM OR SYPHON BREWING

The first known vacuum pot (also known as a syphon) dates back to a drawing of a coffee maker from 1827 created by Professor Norrenberg of Tubingen, Germany. Following on from this there were a handful of patents filed in both Germany and France in the 1830s, many of them submitted by women, culminating in Lyon resident Madame Vassieux's design of 1841, which consisted of a double-globe assembly, with a spigot in the lower globe to dispense the coffee, and a decorative, pierced-metal crown at the top. Amazingly, modern vacuum pots are virtually indistinguishable from Vassieux's 170-year-old design. But besides being an innovative new method for making coffee, it is also thought to be one of the first brewers made from glass, a trend that continued through the 19th century, as glass in general became more readily available in Europe.

HOW IT WORKS

Both vacuum pots and atmospheric pressure pots work across two vessels that can be connected horizontally or vertically by a pipe with some kind of filter arrangement (usually cloth) on the end. The first vessel is set above a heat source and water is added. The second vessel contains the ground coffee. As the water heats in the first vessel, the steam pressure increases and the water is forced through the pipe into the second vessel to mix with the coffee. Once the heat source is extinguished, the pressure in the first vessel drops and pulls the brewed coffee through, filtering out the grounds on the way. In an atmospheric pressure pot, there is a cap on the spout, which is removed, causing the system to pressurize and the brewed coffee to filter through to the lower vessel by gravity alone.

The important point to recognize with all these brewing methods is that the water does not boil. There is sufficient steam pressure created by the hot water to push it from one vessel to the next. In fact, it is nigh on impossible to make the water boil in these devices, since the system is pressurized and the laws of physics prevent it. This is a good thing.

One of the main differences between vacuum brewing and other brewing methods is the consistency of temperature. In a French press, the extraction drops in temperature over time, and in filter brewing, it starts low and increases over time. In both instances, heat is lost to the brewing apparatus, the surrounding air and even the coffee itself. As we know from page 69, brew temperature is an important factor in quality extraction and the syphon is one of the only pieces of equipment that, albeit inadvertently, addresses the topic of stable brew temperature.

The result of this slightly different approach to brewing is, unsurprisingly, a slightly different-tasting cup. Vacuum-brewed coffee tends to pull out more of the dark caramel and rich, nutty characteristics in coffee. This is not to everyone's taste, and often the difference is put down to technique, where it is more likely a product of the brewing temperature.

A

BREWING WITH A VACUUM POT

Makes: 2 cups
Brew ratio: 1:15 (66 g/2 ¼ oz: 1 litre/1 ¾ pints)
Grind: Medium

1 Weigh and grind 22 g/¾ oz coffee.

2 Boil the kettle with fresh filtered water then fill the lower vessel with 330 g (330 ml/11 fl. oz) of water. (**A**)

3 Fit a clean cloth filter to the upper chamber and place the chamber loosely over the lower one, then place the whole unit over a heat source. (**B**)

4 Once the water begins to boil, carefully secure the upper chamber on top (it's important not to fit this too early; otherwise the brewing water will be too cool.) (**C**)

C

B

D

E

5 The boiling water will quickly begin to push upward into the top chamber. The filter can sometimes become dislodged at this stage, producing lots of bubbles, so use a spoon or paddle to centre it.

6 Lower the intensity of your heat source, or move it to one side, but do not extinguish it completely.

7 Add the coffee and give it a good stir. (**D**) (**E**)

8 Give it another stir after 30 seconds.

9 After 60 seconds, extinguish the heat source and allow the coffee to filter down into the lower chamber. (**F**)

10 Pour immediately to prevent the hot glass from scorching the coffee. (**G**) Allow to cool and then enjoy.

F

G

COLD BREWING

Not to be confused with iced coffee (see pages 166–7), cold brewing may seem like a backward kind of approach to a warm cup of coffee, but from a flavour standpoint, there is method in the madness.

Brewing cold results in the extraction of a slightly different range of flavour compounds than those associated with hot brews and similarly, in the drinking of cold coffee we can draw attention to distinct characteristics of coffee origin. Some people find cold brews slightly disappointing since they tend to lack acidity – a result of insufficient heat/energy in the brewing process – but the slant in perspective that they offer over hot brewing methods, for me, makes cold brewing a relevant alternative when exploring coffee's vast dynamic.

Still interested? Great. There are a few different methods around for making cold-brew coffee. Most of them involve a classic filter approach, where gravity slowly pulls the coffee through a paper, metal or cloth filter over time. Now when I say 'time' I mean lots of time – usually over 12 hours. As we know from pages 69–71, rate of extraction is proportionate to heat. Low heat means low energy which, put simply, means things happen more slowly. If you've ever poured cold water over a tea bag by accident, you will have noticed this. In the case of cold brewing, the coffee will literally be materializing drip by drip. You can also use a French press or an Aeropress, or indeed any other brewer that doesn't rely on heat to operate it.

An interesting twist on the cold-brew technique that has proven to curb some of the loss of acidity associated with the method, is to kick-start the operation with a splash of hot water. This initial 'hot bloom' helps with the outgassing of the coffee, but more importantly it improves both the potency and the speed of the early brewing process. Once bloomed, the remainder of the brew is done with cold water.

Once brewed, cold-brew coffee can be sealed and kept in the refrigerator for over a week, then simply heated or poured over ice when the feeling takes you. In light of this, I've noticed that more than a few cafés have started to load their fridges with their own unique cold-brew coffee product, bottled and branded and available for takeaway.

Although there are now a few products available suitable for cold brewing, they all work under similar principles. On the bottom is a collecting vessel that captures drips of brewed coffee; in the middle is a chamber with a filter and the coffee grounds; and on top is a chamber that holds the water, with a valve that controls how quickly it drips into the chamber below.

COLD PRESSURE BREWING

For a slightly more modernist approach to cold brewing, there is the option of using a cream whipper/siphon.

I have been using cream whippers to make infusions for a number of years now, and they have proven to be very useful tools for extracting the flavours of one ingredient into another. In this method, the cream whipper is used like any other immersion brewer, carefully filled with the correct ratio of coffee and cold water. The unit is then sealed and 'charged' with 1–2 cartridges of compressed nitrous oxide (N_2O). The gas itself is flavourless, but the physical effect that it has on the coffee and the water is of great interest to flavour enthusiasts.

It has been calculated that a typical 500 ml/17 fl. oz cream whipper, filled halfway, then charged with two 8-g/^{1}/4-oz N_2O cartridges, would hold a pressure of around 11-bar/160 psi – above even that of an espresso machine (typically operated at 9-bar/130 psi pressure). That's not to say that it is espresso that we're making here, as it is the grind size that characterizes that kind of brewing (here we are using a coarse filter), but the pressure initially exerted on the liquid may be enough to force some of it into the coffee grounds – and then back out again once the pressure is released – to form a more complete extraction.

This all sounds rather great on its own, but there are other forces at work here, too. After the initial pressurising of the vessel, the airspace, liquid and coffee will seek to reach equilibrium. This is where the pressures of all three components are equal and can take some time, depending on how the solution is agitated. Under such immense pressure, nitrous oxide will dissolve into the brewing water (like an unopened bottle of carbonated water) and even into the solid cavities of the coffee itself. Both water and coffee then become highly pressurized materials. When the gas from the unit is quickly released, the coffee and water (crucially in that order) will rapidly depressurize. Suddenly then, for a very short period of time, the coffee is at a higher pressure than the brewing water and is bursting to get out. This is very good news for flavour extraction. The violence of depressurization fractures the coffee on a cellular level, causing a huge and sudden increase in surface area and potential volatile extraction points.

This process is known as nitrogen cavitation, and despite having been used in coffee circles for some three or so years now, for me it remains one of the best untapped potentials for delicious coffee out there, hot or cold.

BREWING WITH A COLD BREW DRIP

This formula makes a concentrate that can be diluted or iced-up to taste.
Brew ratio: 1:5 (200 g/7 oz: 1 litre/1 ¾ pints)
Grind: Fine filter

1 Place the brewer on a set of digital scales. (**A**)

2 Grind 100 g/3 ½ oz of coffee and place it in the cold brewer. (**B**)

A

B

C

3 If you wish to 'hot bloom' your coffee, set the scales to zero and pour 180 g (180 ml/6 ¼ fl. oz) of hot water over the grounds; give the grounds a stir.

4 Fit the chamber on top and set the scales to zero, then add 500 g (500 ml/17 ¾ fl. oz) water, or 320 g (320 ml/11 ¼ fl. oz) if you followed the 'hot bloom' method in step 3 (**C**).

5 Adjust the valve (**D**) so that the water drips about once every second (**E**)

6 The brewing process should take 12–24 hours (**F**).

7 Keep the brewed coffee in the fridge and dilute, or ice, to taste (**G**). I recommend diluting this recipe with two parts water to one part concentrate.

D

E

A WORD ON COLD BREW CONCENTRATES

Your cold brew concentrates will hopefully taste delicious when diluted correctly, but it doesn't have to stop there. If you're finding things a bit flat, you can always try a squeeze of lime to bolster the acidity.

Pining for some sweetness? Try blending some with ice and a touch of agave nectar (10 g/¹⁄₃ oz per 100 g/3 ¹⁄₂ oz of cold brew concentrate) to sweeten it up. Add some single/light cream in there (15 g/¹⁄₂ oz per 100 g/3 ¹⁄₂ oz of concentrate) and you'll have the most delicious 'Iced Latte' you're ever likely to encounter. Crack open some dark or golden rum and add 20 g/³⁄₄ oz per 100 g/3 ¹⁄₂ oz of concentrate to the mix and you've got a delicious post-dinner treat that will keep in the refrigerator for over a week.

F

G

COFFEE-BASED DRINKS AND DESSERTS

09

STRAITS 7

I was first introduced to this espresso-based drink when I was in Singapore, at the famous Oriole's café and roastery. The 'Strait' part of the name is taken from the Singapore Straits, and the seven comes from the use of seven secret ingredients to build the drink. It's unusual to find good cafés deviating from the conventional family of espresso drinks at risk of tampering with the nuances of their cherished product and upsetting the coffee classicists, so I was quite keen to try this one. It turned out to be delicious: fudgy, wholesome and moreish in a very guilty kind of way.

Discerning the ingredients was not all that easy however. Obviously there was coffee in there and water to brew the coffee, but there was also something milky with a sweetness and a lingering spice. I had to ask three different members of staff before I found anyone willing to even entertain the idea of sharing the secrets of the drink, but following an incognito meeting in a dark alley behind the shop, where I persuaded a nervous bartender to write the ingredients down, I left with a scrap of paper with seven scrawled words: coffee, water, milk, condensed milk, salt, pepper and sugar. No quantities, mind you – that bit I had to work out for myself.

INGREDIENTS

SERVES 1

30 g/2 tablespoons condensed milk

100 g (100 ml/3½ fl. oz) whole milk

5 g/1 teaspoon granulated sugar (or to taste)

a pinch of finely ground black pepper

a pinch of fine salt

30 g/1 oz espresso

1 Add the condensed milk, milk, sugar, pepper and salt to a steel jug/pitcher and stir until combined. Leave to one side while you extract the espresso. Steam the milk mixture to 65°C/150°F, then pour into the espresso in your preferred fashion.

2 It should come as no surprise that this drink cries out for a sugary treat to be served alongside it. My personal preference leans towards a nice crumbly shortbread biscuit. Do it now!

STEPHENSON'S IRISH COFFEE

This is the second book in which I have featured an Irish coffee, and if you've read my comments on the drink in *The Curious Bartender: An Odyssey of Whiskies*, you will no doubt find this an ironic turn of events.

My passion for cocktails, whiskey and coffee ought to elevate my personal appreciation of the Irish coffee above all other worldly things. In fact, the opposite is true. I possess such a senseless hostility towards this iconic drink that an Irish bartender presuming to serve me one would be reduced to tears by cold stare alone – did I mention that I am of Irish descent? And so the paradox deepens...

Recently my distaste has developed into a morbid curiosity. It has become a personal mission to make this drink taste good, while at the same time convincing others that the classic version is bad.

You see, on paper Irish Coffee should work. We have the combined powers of fat, sugar, alcohol and caffeine – some of life's greatest pleasures – all working towards a common goal of deliciousness. But in mixing sweetened coffee and whiskey together we discover not a grand unification but an abomination of epic proportions. Nuances are lost, subtleties abandoned and we are left with only wood-flavoured coffee and hot alcohol fumes. The purpose of the cream is to temper the heat of the coffee and the burn of the alcohol – a kind of chilled safety blanket – but the damage has been done and no amount of cream can save us. The problem lies less in the ingredients and more in the execution: balance and ratio have been sacrificed for simplicity and ease of service.

My new recipe is effectively a reverse of the classic where warm whiskey-flavoured cream is floated on top of chilled sweetened black coffee. The effect of warm cream on the lips is far more pleasant than dipping your lip into cold cream on top of a classic Irish Coffee only to have it burnt a moment later by the hot coffee underneath. I have also mixed the whiskey with the cream, rather than the coffee, since together these two have proven a powerful affinity (see exhibit A: Bailey's).

For the coffee I recommend using something a little darker roasted, as it's chocolate, caramel and vanilla characteristics we're looking for here. Brew as iced coffee, or cold drip, then sweeten it slightly in the service of after-dinner appeal.

INGREDIENTS
SERVES 1

FOR THE COFFEE

150 g (150 ml/5 fl. oz) cold drip/ chilled black coffee (see pages 142–5)

5 g/1 teaspoon granulated sugar (or to taste)

FOR THE CREAM

300 ml/10 fl. oz whipping cream

100 g (100 ml/3½ fl. oz) Teeling Single Grain Irish Whiskey

0.8 g/$\frac{1}{32}$ oz xanthan gum

20 g/¾ oz granulated sugar

1 Brew the coffee using your chosen method and sweeten to taste.

2 Use a balloon whisk or a free-standing mixer to whisk the cream, whiskey, xanthan gum and sugar until fully combined and smooth.

3 Carefully lay the cream mixture on top of the coffee using a wooden spoon or a ladle. Alternatively, if you happen to own a 500 ml/ 1 pint cream whipper and a nitrogen oxide (N_2O) cartridge, add the cream to the whipper and charge it with one 8 g/¾ oz N_2O cartridge. Hold the whipper in a warm-water bath or pan at 60°C/140°F, and shake briefly before dispensing onto the surface of the drink.

Note: Both elements of this drink can be stored for a week in the fridge, then built together to order.

COFFEE LIQUEUR

High-strength alcohol has many uses, but one of its better functions is as a solvent. Like water, alcohol relieves coffee of its flavourful compounds, and in many ways it does it better. Alcohol is better at extracting coffee oils, has the ability to form stable emulsions (known as nano-emulsions) with those oils, and is useful in the fight to preserve fragile soluble matter once appropriated. The higher the strength, the better the job it does, so my recipe calls for the strongest alcohol you can get your hands on – don't worry, it's cut down to drinking strength before serving!

The only problem with using alcohol to make coffee is the taste of the alcohol itself. The hot fumes and peppery burn that we associate with ethyl-alcohol do not improve the flavour of a coffee; this is the reason I have never found an enjoyable coffee-flavoured vodka.

One centuries-old workaround to preserve the fleeting flavours of the seasons so that they can be enjoyed all year is the liqueur. By adding sugar to an alcohol extraction, we dramatically lessen the effects of alcohol burn. A 40% ABV liqueur will always slip down a little easier than the same-strength spirit with no sugar. Why it works is not entirely clear, but research suggests the calorie-rich sugar – easily identified by the liquid's viscosity and sweetness – triggers reward mechanisms in our brains, which duly soften the negative effects of alcohol burn. Besides being sweet and tasty, sugar is itself a form a preservative, as jams/jellies demonstrate.

I've explored a range of alcohol-extraction methods over the years, from warm to cold, fine to coarse, long to short, and so on. Certainly some success can be found from using the cream siphon cold-brew method that I detail on pages 138–141. But my current preferred method is a hot bloom using water, followed by a long and slow immersion brew in alcohol.

In the US, look out for the Everclear brand (95 per cent ABV); in Europe, Polish New Make Spirit (also known as Polish Pure Spirit) does the trick. Notice that I have broken with my own convention here and put the alcohol quantity just in millilitres (and fluid ounces). This is because as alcohol strength increases the spirit becomes lighter (a litre of pure alcohol weighs less than 80 per cent that of a litre of water). For this recipe, you need to use the correct volume of spirit, regardless of alcohol strength.

The length of time you infuse the coffee should reflect the spirit strength. My recipe uses Everclear, but I suggest a longer infusion if you want to try lower-strength alternatives.

For the coffee, resist the temptation to use anything too lightly roasted as the subtle finesse of green bean characteristics are notoriously difficult to pick out in the finished liqueur.

Drink this liqueur on its own, use to replace the sugar in an espresso martini, drizzle over ice cream, adulterate a latte, serve alongside chocolates or Tequila, or incorporate into a White Russian cocktail.

INGREDIENTS

MAKES APPROXIMATELY 1 LITRE/1¾ PINTS

100 g (100 ml/3½ fl. oz) filter ground espresso coffee (see page 81)

100 ml/3½ fl. oz hot water

500 ml/17 fl. oz Everclear (95% ABV), or Polish New Make Spirit

300 g/½ cup granulated sugar

200 g (200 ml/6¾ fl. oz) water

1 Add the coffee to a large sealable container, like a Mason jar. Pour the hot water in, allowing it to bloom. After one minute, give the coffee a stir, then pour in the alcohol and stir again.

2 Seal for 12 hours, stirring intermittently. Strain the infusion through a cloth filter a couple of times to remove any particles.

3 Add the sugar and cold water to hit a desirable strength and sweetness, but you should adjust yours based on the spirit you are using.

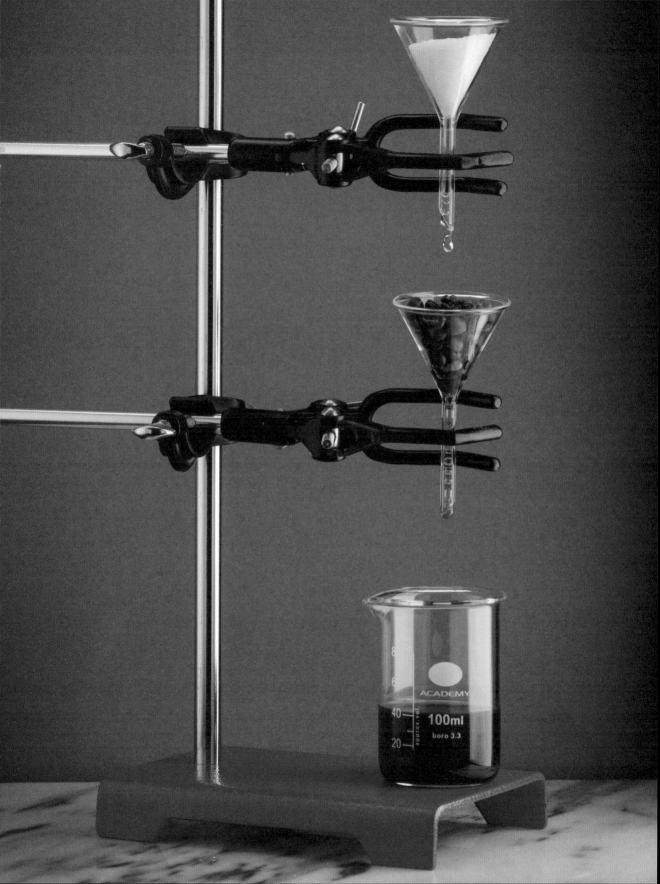

AFFOGATO

The word *affogato* means 'drowned' or 'smothered' in Italian, which neatly sums up the appearance of this dessert-come-drink, as the ice cream slowly sinks beneath a blanket of espresso and its own melted mass. To me, though, this holy matrimony of two of Italy's greatest exports is a culinary unification the likes of which have not been seen since peanut butter and jelly first hit the scene. It's difficult to argue the simple allure of an *affogato*: espresso meets vanilla ice cream; dark and un-diluted meets sweet and light; hot and untempered meets soft and unctuous; volatile and... you get the idea.

As for its origins, those are unclear, but I would hope that the inventors of the drink had the sense to chastise themselves for having not dreamt it up earlier. After all, a world without *affogatos* (*affogati*) would be a much greyer place. In any case, the Oxford English Dictionary first cited the word in 1992. I have found references to the *affogato* in Italian cookbooks and tourism guides from the 1980s, and I even came across an Italian restaurant called Arno's in Houston, Texas, that was serving ice cream and espresso on their menu back in 1979, but I'm sure the practice was widespread – in Italy at least – some time before that.

There are variations on the theme. Some add grappa or whisky; others use a chocolate or hazelnut sauce. In America it was once popular to top it with whipped cream, too. In my mind you can't beat the effortless perfection of the classic, though, where the ritual of eating/drinking the *affogato* becomes marvellous adventure, discovering tiny pockets of what proves to be comparatively bitter espresso, then balancing the taste with the soothing caress of soft vanilla ice cream – each element negating the effect of the previous until they form into a coherent mass of semi-frozen coffee ice cream.

The recipe is a simple as it gets. I would recommend not going too light-roasted with the coffee here, as acidity and brightness prove to be undesirable elements to the piece. The quality of the ice cream, of course, plays a part, but I have found that even the lowliest tub of store-bought frost can be absolved of its crimes with a healthy measure of espresso – in fact, the *affogato* is perhaps the easiest and best way to pimp an otherwise unremarkable ice cream that there is.

INGREDIENTS

SERVES 1

150 ml/⅔ cup vanilla ice cream

double shot of espresso

Dispense the espresso straight over the top of the ice-cream, or decant into a jug/pitcher and serve alongside while still hot.

COFFEE ICE CREAM

Coffee ice-cream was a favourite of mine as a child, and along with coffee cake, likely formed my earliest tentative steps into the glorious world of coffee flavour. These days I rarely indulge in coffee ice cream anymore – once one becomes a coffee geek, it's only natural that coffee-flavoured foodstuffs are treated with a high level of scrutiny, too. Sadly, most coffee ice creams are made from some deplorable food concentrate, quietly covered up by generous helpings of sugar, fat and all manner of other ungodly seasonings.

The easy solution is to make your own ice cream: using better-quality coffee will produce better ice cream. In its most basic form, ice cream is made from a mixture of sweetened cream, ice (derived from the water in the cream) and air. When the mixture is chilled below 0°C/32°F, the water in the cream freezes, leaving behind a gloopy mixture of milk fat, milk solids and unfrozen, sugary water. This stuff coats the millions of ice crystals found in a single scoop and also traps air when the ice cream is churned, leading to the soft and creamy consistency that we all pine for.

In addition to controlling the ratios of sugar, fat, water and flavourings in the mix, other variables can be manipulated to produce ice creams of different properties. By incorporating egg yolk and certain gums (hydrocolloids) we can also control the firmness, elasticity, flavour intensity, length of flavour delivery and even propensity to melt.

My coffee ice cream recipe has been born out countless experiments and aims to celebrate the flavour of the coffee by using no egg and slightly less fat and sugar (making it slightly more healthy). By reducing (or in the case of the egg, removing) these ingredients, I am at risk of producing a more sorbet-like product, so the recipe calls for two thickeners – carageenan lambda and Xanthan gum – which will administer a hefty whack of body and viscosity while contributing no flavour at all. These specialist ingredients are widely available online.

INGREDIENTS

MAKES 2 LITRES/2 QUARTS

110 g/generous ½ cup granulated sugar

0.8 g/^{1}/$_{32}$ oz xanthan gum

1 g/^{1}/$_{32}$ oz carrageenan (lambda class)

2 g/^{1}/$_{16}$ oz salt

450 g (450 ml/2 scant cups) whole milk

100 g (100 ml/3½ fl. oz) fresh espresso

50 g (50 ml/3 tablespoons) double/heavy cream

50 g/1¾ oz cocoa butter

1 Blend the first four ingredients into a fine powder.

2 Pour the milk and warm espresso into a food processor on low speed.

3 While it is still warm, add the dry ingredients.

4 Mix for a further two minutes, then add the cream and cocoa butter.

5 Churn in an ice-cream maker (see below) following the manufacturer's instructions.

Note: By far the easiest way to freeze ice cream is to use liquid nitrogen in a freestanding mixer, such as those made by Kitchen Aid. The accelerated speed offered by liquid nitrogen also makes for smaller ice crystals and a smoother, silkier texture to the finished product.

PUMPKIN SPICE LATTE

For most people, the festive period is all about singing carols, sitting around a tree, and eating inordinate quantities of food with the family. For some people, however, winter has gone over and above the normal level of debauchery and developed into a period of wholly sinister activities. Yes, I'm talking about the pumpkin spice latte, popularized by our old friend Starbucks.

'How can something called a pumpkin spice latte be sinister?', I hear you ask. After all, here is a drink where the name alone paints a picture of candy canes, bunny rabbits and sickly sweet smiles. Delve into the inner workings of this drink, though, and you'll find a harrowing tale of high-fructose corn syrup, caramel colourings, condensed milk, liberal helpings of sugar at every available opportunity – over 50 g/2 oz in the 'Grande' – synthesized spice flavourings, and to top it off, below-par espresso (I'll refrain from reprimanding them for lack of physical pumpkin, as the name clearly states that it is 'pumpkin spice' one should expect in the taste, not a large orange vegetable).

Little wonder that people line up for these things, though; the classic combination of warm sweetened milk with winter spices, pepped up with caffeine, and you have everything the body needs to survive the perils of late-night gift shopping. It's true: fundamentally the flavours work well, which is why you can get away with executing the drink in a lazy fashion and it will still be a great crowd-pleaser. Execute it with an eye for detail, authenticity and flair, however, and you have a genuinely fantastic drink in the making. I set myself the challenge of re-inventing this drink with the aim of both improving the flavour (some might say an impossibility) and making it a little more favourable to the waistline.

My recipe is a somewhat modernist take on the PSL, but well worth the effort of sourcing the ingredients and producing the components as, once done, the drink can be turned out en masse or revisited for an individual serve. Much of the espresso character will be kept in check in this drink, but choose a coffee that is fairly dark to bring some roast character into play.

INGREDIENTS

PUMPKIN SPICE SAUCE

MAKES 1 KG/2 LBS (ENOUGH FOR AT LEAST 30 SERVINGS)

1.5 kg (1.5 litres/2½ pints) whole milk

40 g/1½ oz star anise

20 g/¾ oz ground ginger

15 g/1 tablespoon ground nutmeg

10 g/2 teaspoons black pepper

10 g/2 teaspoons dried orange peel

100 g/3½ oz egg yolks

500 g/1 lb 2 oz caster/granulated sugar

50 g (50 ml/2 fl. oz) dark rum (optional)

MAPLE AND PUMPKIN WHIPPED CREAM

MAKES 370 G/1½ CUPS

200 g (200 ml/2 scant cups) whipping cream

30 g (30 ml/2 tablespoons) maple syrup

20 g (20 ml/4 teaspoons) pumpkin seed oil

0.3 g/a pinch of xanthan gum

SALTED SPICE MIX

2 g/¹⁄₁₆ oz. ground cinnamon

1 g/4 pinches black pepper

1 g/4 pinches ground mace

1 g/4 pinches ground ginger

0.5 g/2 pinches salt

FOR THE PUMPKIN SPICE LATTE

30 g (30 ml/2 tablespoons) Pumpkin Spice Sauce (see left)

30 g (30 mi/2 tablespoons) fresh espresso

180 g (180 ml/²⁄₃ cup) whole milk

1 Start by preparing the pumpkin spice sauce. Put the milk, the spices and the orange peel in a saucepan and simmer on a low heat for 30 minutes, or until the liquid has reduced by half. Strain and discard the spices. Put the egg yolks into a separate bowl and slowly pour the hot spiced milk in while whisking. Finally, add the sugar to the liquid and whisk until fully dissolved. If you wish, finish with a splash of dark rum for additional richness and to preserve shelf-life. Store in the fridge for up to 10 days (with rum) or five days (without).

2 For the whipped cream, whisk the cream on high speed using a handheld blender and add the syrup, ensuring that it is completely mixed in. Next, add the xanthan gum; then, while still whisking, slowly drizzle in the oil; it should take

about a minute. Store the cream in a suitable container in the fridge. Alternatively, if you own a 500 ml/1 pint cream whipper and a nitrogen oxide (N_2O) cartridge, transfer the cream to a siphon and leave to rest for 10 minutes, then charge with a N_2O cartridge. The cream will keep in the fridge for up to a week.

3 For the spice mix, grind all spices and seasoning together in a spice grinder or blender. Store in a sealed container.

4 Mix the pumpkin spice sauce with the espresso and stir well. Steam the milk and pour into the espresso and pumpkin mix. Carefully spoon on the cream, or if you have one, give your cream whipper a brief shake and dispense on top of the drink. Finish with a dusting of spices.

ESPRESSO MARTINI

In a sense, the martini is to cocktails as the espresso is to coffee. An inconspicuous little package of concentrated flavour, loaded with stimulating effect and wicked intent. So I suppose it was inevitable that these two bastions of psychosomatic alteration should one-day combine forces to become allies in the fight for a good night out.

That particular treaty was signed in the 1980s, when – so the story goes – London bartending legend Dick Bradsell, while working at the Soho Brasserie, combined espresso and vodka for a female patron. The early version of the cocktail was actually called 'Vodka Espresso', but as with many of the cocktails invented in the 1980s, it was only a matter of time before it found its way into the iconic martini glass and was renamed 'Espresso Martini'.

Some versions of this drink include a splash of coffee liqueur – Tia Maria or Kahlúa being the usual suspects – resulting in a corruption of the original Espresso Martini and a later iteration of the drink known as the 'Pharmaceutical Stimulant'. I would argue that there's no place for a liqueur in this cocktail; after all, the sugar and espresso components of the cocktail form a pseudo-coffee liqueur anyway. Remember that these off-the-shelf liqueurs are not without their shortcomings when it comes to flavour, either, so if you must, why not make your own (see page 152)?

If you fancy a twist, try swapping the vodka out for aged 100 per cent agave Tequila or rum – Guatemalan rums work particularly well. If using rum you may need to drop the sugar slightly to compensate for the sweetness of the spirit.

For the coffee, I suggest going as light as you dare. A Kenyan one with a nice berry aroma has long been my coffee of choice for this drink.

INGREDIENTS
SERVES 1

30 g (30 ml/2 tablespoons) fresh espresso

50 g (50 ml/2 fl. oz) vodka (I personally like the creaminess of potato-based vodkas in this drink)

10 g (10 ml/2 teaspoons) sugar syrup (or more if you prefer it sweeter), made with a 2:1 ratio of caster/granulated sugar to water, heated until the sugar dissolves.

Add the ingredients to a cocktail shaker filled with ice and shake for at least 10 seconds. Strain into a chilled martini glass.

Note: the classic foam that sits on top of this drink is a result of the carbon dioxide in the espresso forming relatively stable bubbles that are held by the combination of sugar and melanoidins.

CASCARA

It was the team at Square Mile Coffee Roasters in London that first introduced me to cascara, back in 2008. During a brief but rather caffeinated visit to their East End roastery I was offered a glass of cascara as a parting drink. After getting over the surprise of being offered a non-coffee beverage, I duly sipped on the warm rose-coloured liquid. The taste was like a cross between rose hip, green pepper and watermelon – peculiarly vegetal and yet fruity and sweet at the same time. When I asked them what it was, they told me it was cascara – the dried skin and fruit from the dried coffee cherry.

Traditionally the skin and attached fruit are destined for the compost heap, where they will eventually form a part of excellent fertilizer. But process them in the correct manner and cascara (from the Spanish 'husk') makes a pleasant drink capable of carrying through characteristics of the variety and origin of the plant it spawned from.

Perhaps the most interesting thing about drinking cascara is the unprecedented caffeine jolt that it provides. It makes sense, I suppose, since this is a fruit from the coffee tree after all. But on some occasions I have experienced a caffeine buzz from cascara of such a combative nature that it has threatened to suffocate me with nervous paranoia! Recent tests (conducted by none other than Square Mile themselves) showed that cascara actually contains less caffeine than everyone assumed, and less than half that of a typical coffee brew of the same volume.

Regardless of all that, the question still remains, why isn't cascara more widely consumed? It's not like there's a shortage of coffee cherries in the world. Well, it is popular in Bolivia, where it is called *sultana*. In Yemen the tea is known as *qishr* and is likely related to the pre-coffee-beverage practice of chewing on coffee cherries (see page 10). The Yemeni cherry is ground down into a much finer powder than the leathery pieces of cascara you can just discern in the teapot, however; plus it is often seasoned with spices, too.

There's more to just cascara than tea, though. Turn it into a syrup and add soda water for a delightfully refreshing soft drink. Mix it with oats and honey for a delicious caffeine-powered treat. You could even set it into a jelly for coffee-themed parties – everyone has coffee-themed parties, right?

INGREDIENTS

SERVES 1

12 g/2 heaped teaspoons cascara

500 g (500 ml/17 fl. oz) water heated to 90°C/194°F

Brew cascara in a teapot, French press or even straight into a suitable jug/pitcher, as long as you have a tea strainer to filter it with. Stick to a brew ratio of 24 g/¾ oz: 1 litre/1¾ pints.

BUTTER COFFEE

As the developed world trips over itself to renounce the high-carbohydrate diet, we seem to be finding ourselves test subjects in an ever-expanding range of new-age fat- and protein-based meal options. And at the head of the charge is that one-time scapegoat for all things evil: butter. So it stands to reason that someone should mix butter with coffee, as if their proximity to one another on the breakfast table weren't reason enough already.

Before you reach for any old block of butter though, you should know this first: The colour of your butter can be attributed to the diet of the cow that produced it. Studies show that carotenoids, such as beta-carotene – the stuff that gives carrots their colour – are also present in butter produced by grass-fed cows. Carotenoids are known for their antioxidant effects, so the hue of your butter can give some indication as to what the cow was fed on and the carotenoid content of your butter, darker apparently being better.

Sound wrong? Hey, let's not forget that butter is made from milk/cream and we're not so shy about mixing that with our morning brew. Actually, now that I think about it, what we are doing here is re-engineering a latte by blending milk fats into a black coffee.

Of course, fat and water don't mix very well, so some jiggery-pokery may be required. Butter is an emulsion of fat and water, where the water phase (approximately 15 per cent) is trapped within a continuous phase of liquid fat and crystallized fat grains. In normal circumstances, adding butter to coffee causes it to split as the fat network breaks down. Blending briefly helps stabilize the mixture for a short time, but in my recipes I've used soy lecithin, which engineers a true emulsion of butter fat and coffee that will not split and will have a smoother, less greasy texture.

If the recipe below isn't your cup of tea, how about coffee in your butter? It might sound strange, but all the wonderful roasty characteristics of coffee can supercharge the natural nuttiness of clarified brown butter and do a wonderful dance with the brown of a joint of beef or even a burger – it works a treat on toast, too. The recipe is simple: Mix 750 g/1²/₃ lbs clarified butter with 250 g (250 ml/8 ½ fl. oz of hot filter coffee (brewed to your own specifications) then leave it to set harden in the fridge where it will keep indefinitely.

INGREDIENTS

Serves 2

300 g (300 ml/10 fl. oz) black coffee (naturally processed coffee [see page 30], or anything with earthy chocolate characteristics works well)

1.5 g/6 pinches soy lecithin

30 g/2 tablespoons butter (from grass-fed cows)

Combine one-third of the hot coffee with the lecithin using a stick blender (or whisk in a bowl). Blend on a fast setting for 20 seconds, then add the butter and blend for another 20 seconds. Slowly pour the remainder of the coffee in while still blending; it should take another 20 seconds. Sweeten if you like, then serve.

ICED COFFEE

All of us have an opinion on what temperature our coffee should be served at. For most, a sensible degree of heat in a filter coffee is just fine. A bit of temperature assists with the volatilization of aromatics in the mouth. Some people aren't content that their drink is hot enough unless a layer of flesh is stripped from their soft palate. Some, like me, may prefer their coffee slightly cooler, allowing acidity to drop off slightly and body to thicken.

Genuinely cold black coffee, though? That is perhaps a stretch for even for the most experimental among us. But in recent years icing up a filter brew has become all the rage when the sun is shining. While the cynic in me sees the iced coffee trend as an essential hot-weather earner for panicked café operators, iced coffee at its best offers a refreshing, low-calorie beverage, with all the delicious characteristics of the coffee that you love.

It does taste a bit different, however. The colder our tongues get, the harder it is to detect its sweetness. This phenomenon explains is why ice cream is such a delight straight from the freezer, but nauseatingly sweet once it has melted. It also explains why iced coffee has a more pronounced bitterness and less sweetness to back it up – lending itself well to lighter roasted coffee, where we find that as the sweetness drops off, a clean and crisp 'bite' is its replacement.

In terms of brewing technique I would recommend using a paper filter or Aeropress and brewing directly onto ice. Ice adds another variable to the mix, and an important one at that. As your brewed coffee hits the ice, the ice will do what it does so well, and begin to melt. Now, the melt is something that needs consideration before you brew, since the coffee will become diluted and weaker over time. I've heard much discussion on the ratio of ice to brewing water in the past, but in my opinion it is a moot point. The amount of ice you use makes little difference, since unless it is an inordinately small amount, it is highly unlikely that it will melt in its entirety. Also, the melting action of the ice will drop off significantly once the coffee is chilled to near 0°C/32°F. In an ideal world, we would calculate the precise amount of meltage expected before constructing the drink, but this is difficult as it depends on a number of factors: temperature of the ice, temperature of vessel holding the ice, level of insulation provided by the vessel, and whether the coffee/ice mixture is stirred or not.

My approach requires some forward planning, but ultimately results in a consistent drink every single time. You see, the only guaranteed way to overcome the uncertainties of dilution from ice is to chill the coffee with more coffee. By using coffee ice cubes to cool down your coffee, you can have the best of both worlds, chilling and preserving the strength of the beverage at the same time! Oh, and if you're going to the trouble of making coffee ice cubes, be sure to try them with your favourite whiskies, rums and Tequilas!

INGREDIENTS
Serves 1

420 g (420 ml/14 fl. oz) black coffee (brewed with a paper filter [see pages 128–9] or an Aeropress [see pages 134–7])

1 Decant the coffee into ice-cube trays.

2 Cover the trays and allow to cool, then place in the freezer for at least 12 hours.

3 Repeat step 1, scaling the recipe up to the desired quantity, but bearing in mind that the size of the finished drink will increase by at least 50 per cent as the ice melts.

4 Measure 100 g/3½ oz of coffee ice-cubes for every 100 g (100 ml/3½ fl oz) of hot-brewed coffee that you have made.

5 Add the ice cubes to the brewed coffee, then stir for 60 seconds to chill.

10

APPENDIX

COFFEE-PRODUCING COUNTRIES

Over one-third of all the world's countries produce coffee and most of them sit within the tropics of Cancer and Capricorn. Each country produces its own style of coffee, and many have individual regional traits too. Some countries will experience one harvest a year and others two; some have long drawn out seasons, which means they harvest for most of the year round. Over the following pages you will find a brief synopsis of the operations of 40 coffee-producing countries (some of which do not feature on the map opposite, because they fail to reach the commercial criteria listed below, but are still worthy of an honourable mention.)

THE COFFEE BELT

The map opposite includes the countries that are currently producing coffee on a commercial scale (measured as over one thousand 60-kg/130-lb bags a year). Nations are ranked based on their total annual production of green coffee at the time of writing, but the exact standings are prone to shifting as the year's crops come in. The map is also colour coded, indicating whether Arabica, Robusta, or both species are commercially grown in that specific country. Countries that produce both species tend to favour Arabica, however.

COUNTRIES BY PRODUCTION

1 Brazil	**8** Peru	**15** Nicaragua	**22** Madagascar
2 Vietnam	**9** Uganda	**16** Tanzania	**23** Cameroon
3 Colombia	**10** Mexico	**17** Thailand	**24** The Philippines
4 indonesia	**11** Guatemala	**18** Papua New Guinea	**25** Laos
5 Ethiopia	**12** Ivory Coast	**19** Kenya	**26** Ecuador
6 India	**13** Malaysia	**20** El Salvador	**27** Dominican Republic
7 Honduras	**14** Costa Rica	**21** Venezuela	**28** Haiti

COFFEE SPECIES

- 100% Arabica
- Arabica & Robusta
- 100% Robusta

29 Rwanda
30 Democratic
Republic of Congo
31 Burundi
32 Guinea
33 Togo
34 Yemen

35 Bolivia
36 Cuba
37 Panama
38 Sierra Leone
39 USA(Hawaii)
40 Nigeria
41 Angola

42 Ghana
43 Malawi
44 Jamaica
45 Central African Republic
46 Liberia

AFRICA

BURUNDI

Since Burundi is beginning to compete seriously in the speciality coffee arena, it is easy to forget that most of its inhabitants live in relative poverty; in 2013 the country was ranked second in the Global Hunger Index. Coffee is grown throughout Burundi, one of the smallest countries in Africa, and business is focused on 150 or so centralized washing stations. A large number of these are owned by the government (although this is starting to change) and they process the coffee from many, sometimes hundreds, of small, family-run farms. In the past this has raised concern about the ease of traceability, but the authorities are now alert to this and are taking steps to improve the flow of information from farm to roaster. As in neighbouring Rwanda, the bacterial disease known as 'potato defect' has caused enormous disruption in the past but now seems to be coming under control. Expect flavours similar to those found in Rwanda.

ETHIOPIA

Seen by many as the birthplace of coffee, Ethiopia is today perhaps the most exciting producing country in the world. It provides some fantastic coffees from a pot of thousands of natural heirloom mutations of the *typica* variety. Coffee character can range from floral and peachy to sweetly citric, chocolate, Assam tea and heady wild berries. It is certainly worth looking out for coffees from the Harrar region (especially those that have been naturally processed) and the awesome washed coffees of the Yirgacheffe region in the south.

KENYA

Kenya's chief export is tea, which accounts for 21 per cent of the country's total export revenue – almost four times the export income from coffee. What Kenyan coffee lacks in quantity, however, it undoubtedly makes up in quality. It was Kenyan coffee that was responsible for one of my first coffee epiphanies – of which there have been many – and it continues to amaze me to this day. Famed for its juicy red-and-black-fruit acidic characteristics, Kenyan coffee is grown mostly on either large estates or smallholdings in the central and western regions, and tends to consist of washed *typica* hybrids such as SL–28, SL–34 and K7 varieties.

MALAWI

Malawi grows a wide range of coffee varieties, including *catimor* and the famed geisha, which are at the opposite ends of the spectrum in terms of quality. This confusion of identity is a reminder that coffee production is very much in its adolescence in Malawi, one of the smallest producing countries in the world. Considering the diversity of the regions and varieties, however, we may expect to see some wonderful Malawian coffees in the future.

RWANDA

Rwanda has been forced to overcome some terrible events and disasters over the years, not least the genocide of 1994, which claimed the lives of nearly 10 per cent of the entire population. Coffee became a big part of Rwanda's recovery, leading to the emergence of some truly stunning bourbon and Mibirizi (a Rwandan mutation of bourbon) varieties. The cream of the crop has ripe-fleshy-fruit qualities ... but keep an eye out for the notorious Rwandan 'potato defect', caused by a type of bacteria that attacks the coffee cherry.

TANZANIA

As Tanzania shares its borders with every major African coffee-producing country except Ethiopia, it should go without saying that country's own terroir and climate are also perfect for producing coffee. In the north-west of Tanzania, near Lake Victoria, there is widespread robusta production, which makes up around 25–30 per cent of the country's total output. In the east, bordering Kenya, we find estates on the volcanic highlands

Ethiopian women sorting coffee beans by hand at the Bagersh coffee factory in Addis Ababa. Coffee is critical to the Ethiopian economy.

surrounding Mount Kilimanjaro producing some very interesting juicy arabica coffees from largely bourbon, Kent and *typica* varieties.

UGANDA

Uganda is the second-biggest coffee-producing country in Africa after Ethiopia. On the face of it, this seems surprising since high-quality Ugandan coffees are difficult to find. The explanation is that Uganda produces mostly robusta coffee, which is indigenous to the country; it is, in fact, the world's second-biggest robusta exporter after Vietnam. In addition to the typically African high-grown, juicy, washed arabicas, in the west of the country we find some heavier, naturally processed coffees (see page 29) known colloquially as 'drugars'. Washed coffees are called 'wugars'.

ZAMBIA

Zambia is a relative newcomer to the world of coffee, and especially to speciality coffee, having only established a commercial platform for coffee in the past 50 years. The implementation of modern practices can therefore be taken for granted, especially on the larger estates, which account for the lion's share of coffee exports. Zambia can best be described as 'one to watch'. Expect to find fresh fruity acidity in the best examples.

ZIMBABWE

Unlike most producing nations in Africa, Zimbabwe has seen a dramatic decline in coffee production. Annual output has fallen from 15,000 tonnes in the late 1980s to just 500 tonnes in 2013. Production dropped significantly in 2000, when black militants loyal to President Robert Mugabe stormed the farms of white Zimbabwean nationals and seized them. Lots of coffee land was lost in the process and afterwards the international community shunned the idea of buying from the new farmers. The European Union has put forward plans to inject capital into the industry in the hope of reviving it, but there are concerns that many of the coffee plantations are in the eastern highlands on contested land, which the European Union is reluctant to invest in.

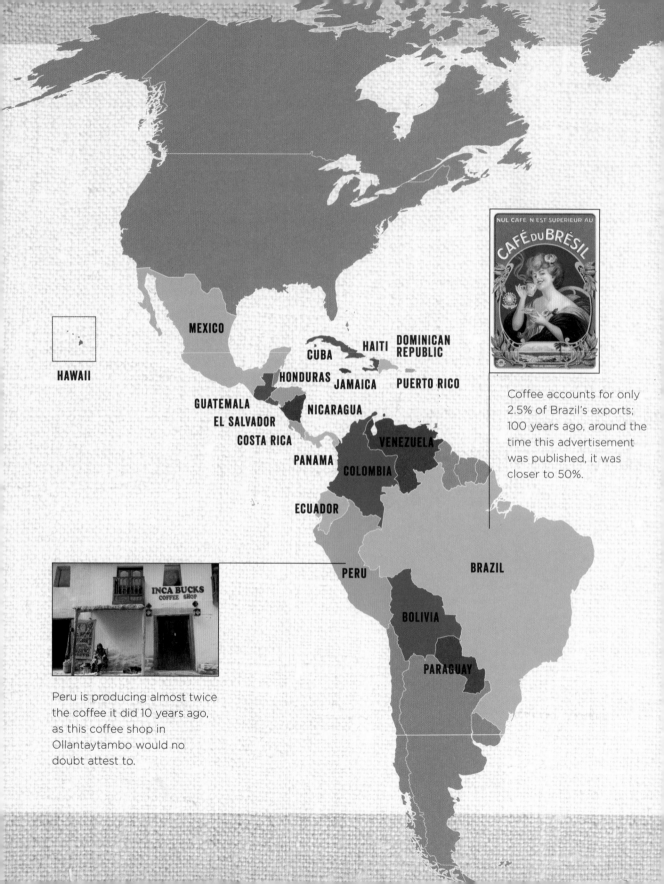

MEXICO

CUBA HAITI DOMINICAN REPUBLIC

HONDURAS JAMAICA PUERTO RICO

GUATEMALA NICARAGUA

EL SALVADOR

COSTA RICA

PANAMA VENEZUELA

COLOMBIA

ECUADOR

HAWAII

PERU BRAZIL

BOLIVIA

PARAGUAY

NUL CAFÉ N EST SUPERIEUR AU

CAFÉ DU BRÉSIL

Coffee accounts for only 2.5% of Brazil's exports; 100 years ago, around the time this advertisement was published, it was closer to 50%.

INCA BUCKS COFFEE SHOP

Peru is producing almost twice the coffee it did 10 years ago, as this coffee shop in Ollantaytambo would no doubt attest to.

THE AMERICAS

BOLIVIA

Bolivia has produced some great coffees in recent years, but the future of this relatively small player looks uncertain as annual production declines. The decline is due partly to the difficulty of transporting crops across the often challenging terrain and partly to the fact that Bolivia is landlocked, meaning that exports generally pass through the ports of Peru. The more lucrative prospects associated with the cultivation of coca (the plant from which cocaine is manufactured) represent another significant threat to Bolivian's already vulnerable coffee industry.

BRAZIL

The world's largest producer since the mid-19th century, Brazil is so closely associated with coffee that the country's very name is almost synonymous with the product. Frank Sinatra was correct when he sang 'They've Got an Awful Lot of Coffee in Brazil'. Export of coffee is worth more than £4 billion/ $6.2 billion a year to Brazil and the Brazilians have become exceptionally efficient at growing it. Coffee farming is almost entirely mechanized, with a 'pick now, sort later' approach, and as such the difference in quality is quite broad. Around 80 per cent of production, which takes place mostly in the south-eastern regions of the country, consists of arabica varieties, and higher-quality examples can be traced to an individual farm (*fazenda*). It is difficult to narrow down flavours from an operation on this scale, but for me it is the buttery, milk-chocolate, nutty, low-acidity examples that keep me coming back.

COLOMBIA

Colombia is an excellent example of how regionality can affect coffee character. The long strip of producing regions that tracks the north-to-south slice of the Andes gives rise to a broad range of arabica styles, from cleanly acidic through to nutty, chocolatey and tropical. In the past, traceability has been an issue, but there have recently been more and more examples of direct trade, and with direct trade come some exceptionally tasty coffees, especially from the southern Nariño region and the central Tolima area. Colombian coffees remain one of the more sought-after and more expensive options in the marketplace.

COSTA RICA

Costa Rica is usually my first port of call when I am welcoming someone into the world of speciality coffee. Robusta was made illegal by the Costa Rica government in 1989, which speaks volumes about this country's commitment to high-quality, high-value coffee. A craft-centred revolution has occurred by which small growers, or collections of growers, have invested in their own wet-milling equipment, allowing them greater control over the processing of their coffee; while roasters enjoy exceptional traceability of product to a particular farm, and in some cases an individual slope, or side, of that farm. Micro-mills have also spawned the range of honey-processing options (see page 31) that the country has become famous for. The diverse range of styles to be found in Costa Rica is certainly worth taking time to explore. Expect to see balanced sweetness in the washed coffees and more funky earthiness in the honey-processed and natural examples.

CUBA

Cuba's coffee production has suffered a sharp decline over the past few decades. According to the UN Food and Agriculture Organization, the total number of hectares where coffee is harvested fell from 170,000 in 1961, following Castro's revolution and the subsequent nationalization of coffee farms, to 26,935 in 2011. Nationalization also meant a poor wage for farmers, and Cubans continue to be among the lowest paid arabica growers in the world. Despite this, the volume of coffee grown in Cuba has tripled in the past three years, and, with the gates (tentatively) opening to foreign investors, it should continue to grow. Such an increase is clearly needed. Up to 80 per cent of the country's home-produced coffee is consumed domestically and coffee imports are still necessary to satisfy demand. Cuba's coffee is mostly arabica and the majority of it is grown in the Sierra Maestra range, which runs along the south-west coast near Santiago.

DOMINICAN REPUBLIC

More coffee is consumed per head in the Dominican Republic than in any other Caribbean island, and most of it is grown domestically. Such a pattern results, more often than not, in a lower-quality product, and the Dominican Republic is no exception to that rule. There some examples of mild, light and floral coffees coming from the midwestern regions on the border with Haiti.

ECUADOR

Although Ecuador has a wonderful coffee-growing climate and certain regions that lend themselves well to the cultivation of high-altitude arabica coffee, around 40 per cent of the coffee grown in the country is robusta. Most of Ecuador's arabicas are relatively poor quality, too; being naturals, they are less sought after by the speciality coffee industry, but interestingly some robustas are wet-processed, resulting in an atypical style for the poorer-quality coffee. Sift through the chaff and you may find some examples of bright and floral arabica coffees from the southern growing regions.

EL SALVADOR

El Salvador has a long history of coffee production and at one time it was the fourth-biggest producer in the world. Memories of political unrest, oppression of the poor, civil rebellion and long periods of military rule – themes that are all too common in this part of the world – still haunt the people of El Salvador, but for the most part the coffee industry has weathered the turmoil. Low-yield, heirloom bourbon varieties grown at altitude are the backbone of El Salvador's well-recognized sweet and juicy cup quality. The Pacas variety was discovered here in 1950 and has since been bred with the Maragogype to create the desirably herbaceous Pacamara variety. El Salvador produces some of the sweetest and complex coffees around, especially from the late-growing region around the Apaneca–Llamatepec mountain range.

GUATEMALA

Coffee, sugar and bananas compete annually for the title of Guatemala's biggest export. The history of the country over a period of 150 years has been inextricably linked to coffee, since coffee was the cause of the mass relocation of indigenous peoples in the late 19th century, and prompted the CIA coup and resulting civil war of the mid-20th century. It would appear that these events have done nothing to affect the quality of Guatemalan coffee, however. With strong regional identities and a generally high standard, Guatemala has produced some of my favourite herbal and fleshy-fruited coffees of recent times. Traceability is generally excellent, so look out for Catuai and Caturra varieties, which are grown near the towns of Antigua and Huehuetenango (pronounced *hway-hwet-en-an-go*).

HAITI

In 1780 Haiti was known as Saint-Domingue and prospered under French colonial rule. At the time it produced more than half of the world's supply of coffee, but these days it accounts for a mere 0.2 per cent. Haiti is a country that has struggled continually with political turmoil and poverty, and more recently with the consequences of natural disasters, but it stands out as a unique example of a nation almost entirely populated by descendants of a slave workforce, who mounted a major revolt in 1804. Deforestation and soil erosion have also been major contributory factors in the decline in coffee production and especially the decline in exports. The potential remains for a successful coffee industry, but it will only be met with governmental support and the installation of proper infrastructure. Most coffees from Haiti are naturally processed, but some areas in the south are exploring the potential of wet processing.

USA (HAWAII)

Growing coffee in a developed country involves higher costs than elsewhere for the payment of labour, infrastructure and, in the case of Hawaii, mechanized harvesting. These higher costs, combined with successful marketing, mean that Hawaiian coffee commands quite a high price, and counterfeit Hawaiian coffee is not uncommon in many parts of the world. The quality of the coffee perhaps falls short of that which is promised by such a price, but the potential certainly remains. Hawaiian coffee is typical of island coffee style, with milk chocolate and low-acidity characteristics.

HONDURAS

Honduras is the biggest producer in the Central American belt and coffee is the country's main export, accounting for around 15 per cent of the total value of national exports. Government support in the past four decades has given a significant boost to the industry. This began with the founding of the Instituto Hondureño (IHCAFE), which has by various means worked to improve the quality of Honduran coffee, including the construction of regional tasting stations, where producers have access to a range of tools for quality assessment. Unfortunately, not enough was done to protect farms from coffee leaf rust, which in 2013 created a state of national emergency In Honduras. In most cases, traceability is good and the bourbon and Caturra coffee varieties are, if you are lucky, bright, candied and juicy in their style.

JAMAICA

The Blue Mountain region of Jamaica, which produces a coffee variety by the same name, is probably the best-marketed growing region in the world. The cool, misty climate provides excellent coffee-growing conditions, but I suspect that a greater diversity of arabica varieties would be needed for Jamaica to produce anything truly stunning, and Blue Mountain is certainly no longer worthy of the attention that it once received. Production is very low and most of it is snapped up

by Japan, with some finding its way into bottles of Tia Maria. Expect to find clean, nutty and mostly unexceptional coffee from Jamaica.

MEXICO

Most Mexican coffee is grown in the south, with arguably the best coming from the state of Chiapas, which borders Guatemala. There are signs that, in imitation of its neighbour, Mexico is capable of producing top-quality speciality coffee, although most of today's production is destined for the USA. Look out for chocolate, caramel, stone fruit from some of the southern growers, then lighter-bodied, more citrus-flavoured coffees as you head north.

NICARAGUA

The Nicaraguan government has in recent years enthusiastically encouraged farmers to adopt good growing practices – hardly surprising, since coffee remains the country's chief export. In fact, there are very few countries that are so dependent on coffee as Nicaragua; when coffee prices crashed at the beginning of the 21st century, three Nicaraguan banks crashed along with them. The Nicaraguan people have also made their voices heard. In 2010 they took to the streets in an attempt to ban robusta, but were unsuccessful. The recognition that quality is the key to getting good prices is paramount, and farms are starting to show some off some nice complex, fruity coffees to the world. Traceability remains a significant problem, however, because most farms sell on to large wet mills for processing,

PANAMA

Panama shot to fame in 2004 when one of its farms, Hacienda La Esmerelda, won the 'Best of Panama' coffee competition and went on to sell one lot of coffee for a record-breaking $20/£12.75 per pound. Since then, the estate, which is run by the Peterson family, has won the same competition almost every year and the price of its coffee has risen dramatically, with one lot selling for $350/£225 per pound in 2013. The geisha variety, grown by the Peterson family, is now quickly spreading around the world as farmers recognize the potential value of such plants. The coffee is not universally popular, however; its taste is very light, floral, citrusy and tea-like. As for Panama itself, the country is becoming popular with American citizens wanting to purchase a holiday home, a development that threatens to chew away at coffee-producing farmland in what is ironically one of the best producing countries in the world. In response to this, total production has dropped by 15 per cent in the past three years.

PARAGUAY

A relatively small player in the coffee game, Paraguay generally turns out no more than 20,000 60-kg/130-lb) bags in a year, which is less than even some middle-sized estates in neighbouring Brazil. This hasn't always been the case. Output peaked in the 1970s and then dwindled until the coffee crisis of the 1980s, when it dropped off a cliff. What little

coffee is still grown tends to be along the Brazilian border. Transport difficulties, minimal governmental support and poor infrastructure mean that the standard is fairly poor.

PERU

Small farms, mostly organic soils and high altitudes are the main themes in Peruvian coffee production. Peru produces some of the cheapest organic arabica on the market and the quality and consistency of these coffees are improving, too – an excellent trend, since Peru has the potential to produce some outstanding coffees. The biggest growing region is in the north, in Cajamarca state, which accounts for around 70 per cent of all the Peruvian arabica, and, considering that Peru is the ninth biggest coffee-growing nation in the world, that's quite a lot. Inconsistencies aside, Peruvian coffee is generally light, very bright, clean and sweet, but occasionally lacking in powerful fruitiness.

PUERTO RICO

Coffee cultivation is becoming increasingly scarce in Puerto Rico, and the Caribbean island now stands as one of the smallest producers in the world, filling only 700 bags in the 2013 harvest – small enough not to feature in some official statistics. The reasons for this drop are numerous, including the rising costs of seeds and fertilizer, but a crucial factor is the lack of pickers, which means that over a third of the ripe coffee cherries are never even picked.

VENEZUELA

Very little coffee actually leaves Venezuela. Annual production during the past 30 years has held firm at around one million bags, but more and more of it has been destined for domestic consumption. This is mostly a consequence of the strict regulations imposed by the Chávez government in 2003, which saw exports drop from 50 per cent to 2 per cent of the annual crop over the period from the early 1990s to present day. As such, Venezuelan coffees are not easy to come by.

ASIA AND AUSTRALASIA

AUSTRALIA

Apart from the state of Hawaii, Australia is the only economically advanced country that grows coffee commercially. The amount is tiny, however, and it consists entirely of modern arabica varieties. The cost of labour in Australia is much higher than that in less developed countries, meaning that the coffee, which is grown in high-altitude areas along the eastern coast, is mostly harvested mechanically.

CHINA

Coffee is not a huge part of China's economy, but the industry there is growing year by year, producing 82,000 tons in 2013. This figure is expected to increase by 50 per cent in the next five years as new parts of the Yunnan province (famous for its Pu'er tea) in the south are made available for coffee crops, but the infrastructure will need to see some improvements in order to handle it. Arabica coffee from Yunnan is, like the tea, savoury, nutty and of low acidity, produced from mostly *catimor*, bourbon and *typica* varieties.

INDIA

Like some of the other Asian producing countries, India produces a large quantity of robusta coffee as well as higher-quality arabicas. The growing region is in the south, whereas the tea tends to be grown further north, where the climate is slightly cooler. One type of coffee that will always be associated with India is Monsoon Malabar, whose name refers to the practice of wetting the green coffee so that it swells – something that used to happen naturally during the wet months of the year. The process is done with natural coffee and has the effect of amplifying the already wild and heavy character traits of the style. Good-quality arabicas from India are beginning to appear and the industry is exploring a wide range of varieties.

INDONESIA

Indonesia was one of the very first countries to grow coffee commercially, preceded only by Yemen. The country consists of a multitude of islands and it doesn't take long to discover that each island has its own own interpretation of the Indonesian style – best demonstrated in such famous producing regions as Java, Sumatra and Sulawesi, which collectively account for over seven per cent of the world's total coffee production, placing Indonesia third in the running order. Many of the arabica varieties here are subjected to a pulped-natural process, known locally as *giling basah*, typically culminating in a deep, earthy, low-acidity style, and it can perform nicely as part of an espresso blend. The better (washed) coffees from Sulawesi exhibit more of a spicy, fruity character, but retain the Indonesian heavy body.

NEPAL

Although Nepal produced no more than 5,000 60-kg/130-lb bags of arabica coffee in 2013, this was almost double the amount of the previous year and ten times that produced 20 years ago, indicating that output may continue to grow in future. In recent years, many farmers have been attracted to coffee, which can earn them up to three times as much as maize, millet and other commodity crops. Coffee consumption in the capital city, Kathmandu, is even beginning to challenge that of tea.

PAPUA NEW GUINEA

Coffee production in Papua New Guinea is thought to have its genesis in seedlings of Jamaican Blue Mountain planted in the 1920s. Today, it is estimated that over 30 per cent of the population of Papua New Guinea rely on coffee for their income, 99 per cent of which is arabica. The best coffee comes from the eastern highlands near the small town of Goroka, which at its best produces aromas of vanilla tobacco, cedar and tropical fruits from *typica*, *mundo novo* and bourbon varieties.

THE PHILIPPINES

At the beginning of the 19th century, the Philippines was the fourth-largest coffee grower in the world and, since robusta was not officially identified until the 1890s, we can be sure that every bean was an arabica. Oh, how things have changed. These days the Philippines produces mostly robusta and *liberica* varieties, the latter of which is known locally as *kapeng barako*.

THAILAND

Thailand grows almost exclusively robusta coffee destined to be turned into instant coffee, but there is a small amount of washed arabica grown in the northern regions of Chiang Rai and Chiang Mai. Good farming practices and an organic approach to agriculture in these regions have rewarded farmers with very low-defect coffee (including *caturra*, *catuai*, *catimor* and geisha varieties) that in darker roasts produce sweet, fruity flavours and a unique incense-like flowery fragrance.

TIMOR-LESTE

Coffee production in Timor-Leste fell by 10 per cent to 20 per cent a year between 2011 and 2013, suggesting an uncertain future for this country's small industry. Timor-Leste shares the island of Nusa Tenggara with Indonesia (with which it parted company in 2002), and the hilly, craggy landscape lends itself very well to the growing of arabica coffee, but economic survival is a struggle for this poverty-stricken nation. The Starbucks company buys a substantial proportion of the national crop for its Arabian Mocha Timor blend. Coffee is Timor-Leste's biggest cash crop, so it should hopefully play a positive part in the development of this threatened young country.

VIETNAM

It surprises most people to learn that Vietnam is the second-biggest coffee grower in the world. It still produces less than half the volume of Brazil, and the vast majority is lower-quality robusta coffee. But, although only five per cent of Vietnam's crop is arabica, the enormous scale of the industry means that production is more than double that of Kenya. Various small areas dotted around the north of the country offer the necessary altitude that arabica needs, but high-quality examples remain elusive.

YEMEN

Yemen has grown coffee commercially for a longer period than any other nation, and it continues to produce some surprisingly good naturals (naturally processed coffee) from its hilly areas close to the eastern coastline of the Red Sea. Almost all the coffee grown in Yemen is from very small holdings, averaging no more than 500 trees and perhaps 160 kg/350 lb of coffee per season. Unfortunately, this means that traceability is more or less non-existent, with some *typica* varieties sharing their name with a region but not necessarily corresponding with the area in which the coffee was grown. It is also common to see 'Mocha' on Yemeni coffee labels, referring to the port city from where the coffee has been shipped. Expect to find benchmark naturals with volatile fruity qualities.

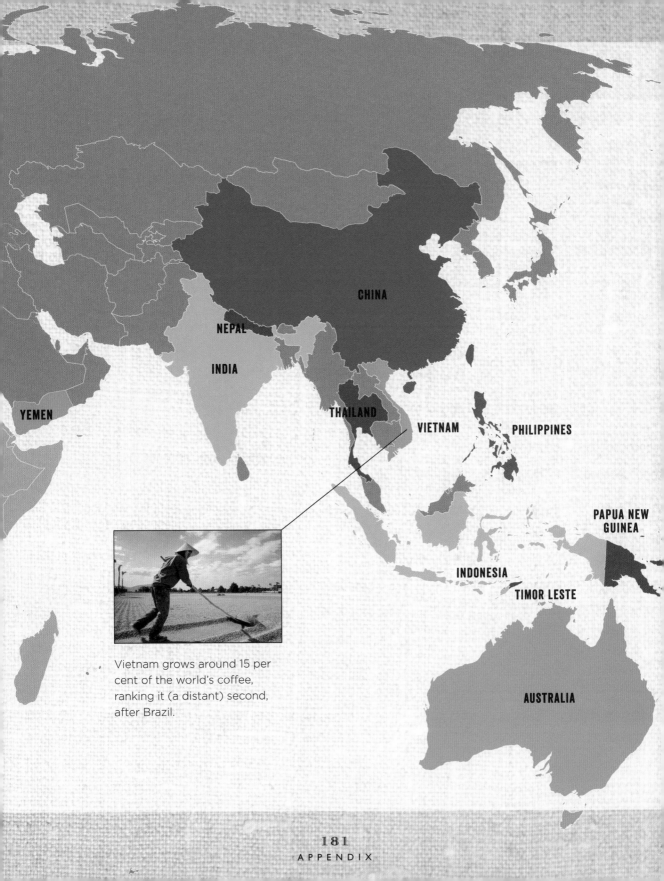

YEMEN

CHINA

NEPAL

INDIA

THAILAND

VIETNAM

PHILIPPINES

PAPUA NEW
GUINEA

INDONESIA

TIMOR LESTE

AUSTRALIA

Vietnam grows around 15 per
cent of the world's coffee,
ranking it (a distant) second,
after Brazil.

VARIETIES OF COFFEE BEAN

TYPICA

Typica is the blueprint for all other arabica varieties. It is thought to have originated from the southern Sudan before flourishing in Ethiopia and eventually being cultivated for commercial production in Yemen in or around the 7th century AD. *Typica* was transported to the East Indies by the Dutch and was also the first variety to cross over to the West Indies, where it was planted on Martinique by Gabriel de Clieu in 1720.

Typica produces red fruit when it is ripe. It is a relatively low-yield variety and has very little resistance to disease, but its cup quality remains popular throughout the world.

The following is an incomplete list of mutations, selections and hybrids of typica that are commonly found in delicious bags of speciality coffee. You will note that, for the most part, I have used only vague tasting notes. Although some varieties are distinguished by obvious character traits, it is impossible to be 100 per cent certain that these will make it though to the cup, since many other factors (including the processing method and roast) must be taken into account when assessing taste.

This list (with the exception of geisha) makes little reference to the numerous wild heirloom varieties of Ethiopia, which are natural cross-breeds between different indigenous varieties. Some of these may involve other indigenous coffee species too (known as interspecific hybrids), which makes for a more diverse gene pool – a fact that is reflected in the character of Ethiopian coffee.

BOURBON

The original *typica* mutation from Réunion (Bourbon) Island, bourbon is the father and grandfather of numerous other popular Latin American varieties, including *caturra*, *catuai*, *pacas* and *mundo novo*. Bourbon is still popular in Latin America today, and has also travelled back to Africa, where it is grown in Rwanda and Burundi. Most bourbon varieties produce red ripe fruit, but there are yellow and orange variations, too. Bourbon is around 20–30 per cent higher-yielding than *typica* and produces coffee of a similar, albeit slightly sweeter and sometimes better balanced style.

CATIMOR

Not to be confused with *caturra* or *catuai*, *catimor* is a hybrid of *caturra* and *timor*. It is a highly disease-resistant strain that was planted widely in Latin America during the 1980s for its ability to fend off coffee leaf rust. Regrettably, though, it lacks the finesse of other arabica cultivars. This is accounted for by the *timor* variety (also known as *arabusta*), which is a natural hybrid between arabica (*typica*) and robusta; the robusta element explains the plant's resilience against disease.

CATUAI

A hybrid of *caturra* and *mundo novo*, *catuai* is a highly disease-resistant, high-yield variety that was developed in Brazil in the 1950s. Just like *caturra*, ripe *catuai* cherries can have either red or yellow pigmentation (I prefer the former). *Catuai* is known for its bold acidity and is a popular variety across most of Central America.

CATURRA

This mutation of bourbon was found near the town of Caturra, in Brazil, in the 1930s. *Caturra* is a higher-yielding, more compact plant that makes for easy picking, but can become its own worst enemy in lower-altitude growing conditions, where the coffee becomes quite light-bodied and the weight of fruit alone can kill the plant. When grown at higher altitudes (above 1,200 m/4,000 ft), *caturra* plants produce both a better-quality coffee and a more sensible yield size. *Caturra* is a common variety in the Central American belt.

GEISHA

With its slightly elongated fruit and leaves, geisha is a mutation of *typica* that is believed to have originated from the south-west Ethiopian town of Gesha (both the spellings *geisha* and *gesha* are acceptable) In the 1930s some seeds were sent to Tanzania, and from there on to Costa Rica in the 1950s. Those two countries remain the only significant cultivators of geisha outside Panama – the country with which it is best associated.

In high-altitude regions of Panama, geisha has proved to be the undisputed queen of varieties, producing coffee with tropical, citrus and tea characteristics. For this reason, we can expect in the future to see many more examples of geisha filling bags of coffee from other countries.

MARAGOGYPE

This variety is considered to be a natural mutation from *typica*. It was first discovered near Maragogipe (with an 'i') in Brazil's Bahia region. *Maragogype* is well known for producing very large beans and makes up half of the *pacamara* variety.

MUNDO NOVO

A bourbon and *typica* hybrid discovered in the 1940s that remains quite popular in Latin America today. It is more disease resistant and better yielding than bourbon and *typica*, but at the sacrifice of some complexity of flavour.

PACAMARA

One of the more sought-after varieties, *pacamara* is a hybrid of *pacas* and *maragogype* that was created in El Salvador in the late 1950s. Just like *maragogype*, it lacks in yield what it makes up for in bean size; its beans are regularly twice the size of a standard bourbon seed. *Pacamara* is highly prized for its quality, showing nice, clean acidity and floral characteristics, especially when grown at higher altitudes.

PACAS

A natural mutation of bourbon, discovered in El Salvador in 1949, *pacas* is a compact plant that can

ABOVE Yellow bourbon lives up to its name, displaying bright yellow, ripe fruit.

withstand relatively low elevation conditions, which is why it was chosen to breed with the contrasting *maragogype* variety.

TEKISIC

Also known as 'improved bourbon', *tekisic* is a dwarf variety that was the result of 28 years of ongoing unnatural selection of bourbon plants conducted by the Salvadoran Institute for Coffee Research (ISIC) between 1949 and 1977. The lengthy process culminated in a relatively low-yield variety that was capable of producing some stunningly complex coffees with a big mouthfeel to back them up. As such, it has been welcomed by some El Salvadorian, Honduran and Guatemalan farms which are striving to improve the quality of their coffee.

SL-28

The 'SL' in SL-28 stands for Scott Laboratories, the name of the technical firm that the Kenyan government employed in the 1930s to identify the native coffee varieties that were best suited for widespread cultivation. It's SL-28 that is partly responsible for the intense blackcurrant character that defines Kenyan coffees from some regions. SL-28 performs best at high altitudes.

SL-34

This variety is the slightly inferior (but by no means bad) sister of SL-28, which also possesses some striking acidity and berry-fruit qualities. SL-34 does a better job than its numerically lower sister at lower elevations, and is resistant to high rainfall at high altitudes, so certainly has its uses. Like SL-28, it is a variety that is quite susceptible to coffee leaf rust.

VILLA SARCHI

This dwarf variety is a bourbon mutation, discovered in Costa Rican town of Sarchi. Branches form at a steep angle from the tree's body and can produce interesting bronze-coloured leaves among the normal green ones. Even more interesting is the excellent fruity coffee that the variety produces, with the added bonus of high yields and reasonable disease resistance.

LEFT A Typica tree in Mexico with ripe coffee cherries ready for picking.

COFFEE-BUYING GUIDE

Just as a carrot or a cucumber deteriorates from the moment it is picked, the quality of a coffee bean diminishes from the time it was roasted. Knowing when your coffee was roasted is fundamental to understanding how fresh it is, so avoid buying bags that don't have a roast date stamped on them. Pre-ground coffee should be avoided too, because, just like chopped vegetables, it spoils at a much faster rate. In recognition of this, many speciality coffee roasters no longer sell pre-ground coffee, but if you must buy pre-ground – the only acceptable excuse being that you are travelling without a grinder or your grinder is broken – it should be freshly roasted, ground and packaged in front of you, and consumed within 24 hours of grinding.

Understanding how the coffee is intended to be brewed is the next important factor. Espresso coffee will generally be labelled as such, usually being of a darker roast and most of the time a blend of different coffees. The unforgiving nature of espresso brewing requires that the coffee flavour be carefully balanced to avoid the exaggeration of some of the coffee's more wayward features in the finished cup. This is done with usually two or three component coffees, like a whisky blend, that cast a smooth crescent of fruity, earthy, bright, sweet, bitter, nutty, floral and roast characteristics. Single-origin espresso coffees are becoming more commonplace now, however, and these coffees are selected for their more placid nature.

Coffees intended for brewing by a more traditional method tend to be lighter-roasted to accentuate acidity, and usually the product of a single country, co-operative or estate. Like a malt whisky, they are the product of a certain place, time and processing method and in general offer a more diverse range of coffee styles than that of an espresso blend.

Lighter-roasted coffees can be brewed as espresso, but this tends to be done only with low-acidity beans. Darker-roasted coffees can be brewed in the traditional manner, but a higher-acidity coffee is usually required to attain the 'brightness' that we would hope to get from this type of brewer.

I never like to keep an open bag of coffee for more than 3–5 days, no matter how well it has been stored. Buy regularly and in small quantities, or consider subscribing to a regular delivery from a roaster, which can be a fantastic route to the discovery of new and exciting coffees.

A fresh bag of coffee, roasted in a style that will complement your chosen brewing method, will set you on the right path. Beyond this, there is a whole world of coffee origin, processing and varieties to explore. The only piece of advice that I will give you is to be as adventurous as possible and continue to challenge yourself with interesting coffees that stretch the boundaries of coffee style.

KOPI LUWAK

The legend of kopi luwak goes back to the 18th century, when the Dutch-controlled Indonesia. The native workers at the time were forbidden from harvesting and selling coffee for their own use, so they took to searching around for it on the forest floor. They found clumps of raw coffee seeds in the faeces of the luwak, a nocturnal civet cat, that had taken coffee cherries as its chief source of nutrition. This civet-poo coffee proved to be delicious once roasted, because the cat selected only the ripest cherries for its midnight snacks and because its digestive system did a fantastic job of stripping the mucilage off the beans.

Jump forward 300 years and kopi luwak still commands a great deal of attention, mostly, it seems, for the novelty of paying a lot of money for something extracted from animal droppings. It should go without saying that, by the standards of today's speciality coffee, kopi luwak coffee does not live up to its price tag, but there is also a far more sinister side to this story that needs to be told.

The market value of kopi luwak is so high that some unscrupulous types have taken to caging these solitary animals in large groups and force-feeding them coffee cherries of all types, ripe, underripe and overripe. There are also many fake versions available. Please avoid kopi luwak altogether and spend your money on some genuinely good coffee that didn't have to pass through a caged animal to get to you.

GLOSSARY

AA Green bean grading that is commonly used in Africa. AA beans will pass through a Grade 18 ($^{18}/_{64}$-inch diameter) sieve perforation, but not a Grade 16, and are among the largest beans. Roughly equivalent to a Superior or Supremo.

Altura Meaning 'height' in Spanish and sometimes used to indicate coffee grown at altitude.

Arabica (*coffea arabica*) The most widely grown coffee species on the planet.

Aromatic (compound) A chemical mixture that contributes to the aroma of coffee.

Bloom The process of pouring a small amount of water over ground coffee – usually in pour-over/ percolation brews – to kick off the extraction. Named after the manner in which the coffee swells as the water penetrates it.

Brew ratio The ratio of brew water to coffee (in grams) that is used in coffee brewing (e.g., 15:1, where 15 times the weight of water is used to coffee weight).

Brew time The total length of time that coffee is in contact with water during brewing.

Burr (grinder) One of the serrated cutting discs used in a burr grinder. The distance between the discs can be adjusted to achieve the desired grind size.

Carrageenan A thickening or gelling agent extracted from red seaweed (Irish moss).

Caramelization A reaction involving sugars that occurs during coffee roasting. A caramelized sugar is less sweet but has greater complexity of flavour and aroma.

Cinnamon roast A very light (cinnamon-coloured) roast dropped on or very shortly after first crack.

City roast A medium roast somewhere between first crack and second crack.

Co-operative (co-op) A group of farms that share resources and infrastructure.

Crack An audible cracking or snapping sound during roasting in two distinct phases of the roast.

Cultivar A portmanteau of the words 'cultivated' and 'variety'; used in references to a coffee variety that has been cultivated for commercial production.

Cup of excellence An annual evaluation programme held in several different countries that aims to source, evaluate and score top-quality coffee, then sell the winning coffees by auction.

Cupping A systematic method of tasting and assessing a selection of different coffees.

Dry mill A place where parchment coffee is hulled, sorted, graded and packed for shipping.

Dry process(ing) After harvest, the whole intact coffee cherry is dried before being hulled to remove the green coffee bean.

Excelso Green-bean grading that is used in South America and particularly Colombia. Excelso beans will pass through a Grade 16 ($^{18}/_{64}$-inch diameter) sieve perforation, but are too large to fit through a Grade 14.

Extraction The capture of soluble material from ground coffee into water during brewing.

First crack The audible popping or snapping noise that emanates from the beans during roasting, and after which the coffee can be considered 'roasted'.

French roast A very dark roast that has passed second crack.

Full city roast A roast that is quite dark; just on the cusp of second crack.

Giling basah A coffee-processing method commonly seen in Indonesia. In this process the coffee is hulled from its parchment before it has been fully dried; this is followed by a drying phase. The result is a full-bodied, quite earthy coffee.

GrainPro A multi-layered plastic bag with a gas barrier used for transporting green coffee. The bags have been shown to extend the flavour life of the coffee significantly over storage in jute or burlap bags.

Green coffee The dried and processed seed of the coffee fruit in its unroasted form. Named for its typically green colour.

Heirloom (varieties) A traditional variety of coffee that is indigenous to, or has been grown in, a specific region for a very long time.

Honey process *see* Pulped natural.

Hulling The final step before storing at the dry mill where the green coffee bean is removed from the parchment shell.

Hybrid A natural or artificial cross-breed of two different varieties or species of coffee plant.

Leaf rust A rust-coloured fungus that attacks the leaves of coffee trees and eventually kills them.

Lot The specially selected batch of green coffee of a specific size.

Maillard reaction An important reaction in coffee roasting that gives coffee its brown colour and many of its associated flavours.

Micro-lot A small selection (typically ten 60 kg/ 120 lb bags or less) from a specific farm or co-op.

Moka/Mokha/Mocha Moka (pot) is a stove-top coffee-maker that produces a strong drink using steam-powered percolation. Mokha is the Yemeni trading port through which, at one time, nearly all the world's coffee passed. Mocha (mochaccino) is a cross between a cappuccino and a hot chocolate.

Monsoon(ing) A traditional method of ageing green coffee in India where the coffee is exposed to wet conditions for approximately three months, resulting in a loss of acidity.

Mucilage The sticky layer of fruity material that surrounds the unprocessed coffee bean.

Mutation A coffee plant that is a descended from another single-variety plant, but shows a marked deviation in terms of height, leaf shape, disease resistance, etc.

Overextraction The capture of too much soluble material during coffee brewing, resulting in a cup that is bitter, astringent, harsh and flat. The cause is usually an overlong brew time or too fine a grind.

Parchment (coffee) The protective shell that still surrounds a green coffee bean after the wet-milling process. The parchment is removed at a dry mill before sorting.

Peaberry A single (typically rounder) coffee seed that forms in a cherry in the place of two.

Percolate The gradual filtration of water through coffee.

Portafilter The handled part of an espresso machine that holds the filter basket, into which ground coffee is placed.

Pre-infusion The initial low-pressure burst of water applied by an espresso machine before proper high-pressure extraction ensues.

Process(ed) A general term that refers to the removal and/or drying of the skin and fruit of the coffee cherry.

Pulped natural After harvest, the coffee beans are squeezed from the cherry then dried on patios or raised beds with their mucilage intact.

Second crack An audible popping or snapping noise that emanates from the beas during the later stages of a dark roast.

Semi-washed *see* Pulped natural.

Silverskin The very fine papery layer of material found on green coffee.

Single origin An ambiguous term that generally refers to a coffee that is not blended and may come from a single country, region, co-operative or estate.

Supremo Green-bean grading that is used in South America. Supremo beans will pass through a Grade 18 ($^{18}/_{64}$-inch diameter) sieve perforation and are the next size up from an Excelso. Roughly equivalent to a Superior or AA.

Strictly high grown (SHG) An indication that the coffee has typically been grown at an altitude above 1,000 m/3,200 ft, which correlates to higher-density (better-quality) coffee.

Tamping A process in espresso brewing where the ground coffee is levelled and compacted in the portafilter basket using a tamper, for an even extraction.

Terroir The environment in which the coffee is grown, including such factors as soil, topography and climate.

Underextraction This is the capturing of too little soluble material during coffee brewing, resulting in a cup that is sharp, sour and weak. The cause is usually too short a brew time or too coarse a grind.

Vienna roast A roast that is dumped at around second crack. This is a dark roast where most of the character of the green coffee will have been lost.

Washed process After harvest, the coffee beans are squeezed out of the cherry, then their sticky mucilage is broken down through an enzymatic process. The mucilage is then washed off and the bean is dried on patios or raised beds.

Wet mill A station or facility that processes coffee cherries into dry parchment coffee.

Wet process *see* Washed process.

Xanthan gum A thickening agent secreted by the bacterium *Xanthomonas campestris*.

INDEX

ACKNOWLEDGMENTS

Not for the last time, I think, I must thank my wife for her patience during the many weeks of research, writing and caffeinating (not in that order) that made this book possible.

Also to my son, Dexter, who is currently accepting challenges for the title of 'youngest barista in the world'!

Thanks to Linda and Rod for allowing me to commandeer their office space for a not-insignificant period of time.

A shout-out to Origin Coffee in Cornwall and Workshop Coffee in London for use of their space, equipment, coffee and expertise.

Thumbs-up to all the people I have enjoyed a coffee with over the years. There're too many of you to remember, but here's a shortlist of names: Anette Moldvaer, Colin Harmon, Dan Fellows, Dave Jones, Flavio Urizzi, Gary McGann, Gwilym Davies, James Hoffmann, Lance Turner, Hugo Hercod, Phil Gevaux, Sam Hebburn, Stephen Morrissey, Tim Williams and Tom Sobey.

Huge thanks once again to the dream team responsible for putting this book together: Nathan Joyce, Julia Charles, Leslie Harrington, Geoff Borin, Addie Chinn and Sarianne Plaisant.

PICTURE CREDITS

All photography by Addie Chinn, with the following exceptions:

Page 8 Wellcome Library, London; Page 11 Palestine Exploration Fund, London, UK/Bridgeman Images; Page 12 © Christie's Images/Bridgeman Images; Page 13 Photo by Rischgitz/Getty Images; Page 14 Mary Evans Picture Library; Page 15 INTERFOTO/Alamy; Page 16 Mary Evans Picture Library/Alamy; Page 18 Mike Greenslade/Alamy; Page 19 Image Courtesy of The Advertising Archives; Page 21 Jake Curtis/Getty Images; Page 22 Philippe Bourseiller/Getty Images; Page 24 World History Archive/Alamy; Page 26 Nick Gunderson/Getty Images; Page 27 Bjorn Holland/Getty Images; Page 28 © Nigel Cattlin/Visuals Unlimited/Corbis; Page 29 © Paulo Fridman/Corbis; Page 31 © Devon Stephens/Alamy; Page 33 Pphoto by Michael Tsegaye/Bloomberg via Getty Images; Page 34 Dallas Stribley/Getty Images; Page 35 © National Geographic Image Collection/Alamy; Page 36 RGB Ventures/SuperStock/Alamy; Page 37 INTERFOTO/Alamy; Page 38 Neil Overy/Getty Images; Page 39 Image Courtesy of The Advertising Archives; Page 40 Jake Lyell/Alamy; Page 41 above left Media for Medical/UIG via Getty Images; Page 41 above right Simon Rawles/Getty Images; Page 46 below left Hulton Archive/Getty Images; Page 46 below right photo by Haeckel collection/ullstein bild via Getty Images; Page 48 istock images; Page 49 © English Heritage; Page 89 left Steve Hamblin/Alamy; Page 89 right ERIC LAFFORGUE/Alamy; Page 116 Irina Zavyalova/Shutterstock; Page 125 © amana images inc./Alamy; Page 132 © Neil Setchfield/Alamy; Page 133 © Image Republic Inc./Alamy; Page 173 © Wolfgang Kumm/dpa/Corbis; Page 174 left © Ian Wood/Alamy; Page 174 right © Found Image Press/Corbis; Page 181 insert © Julian Nieman/Alamy; Page 183 © HUGHES Herve/Hemis/Corbis.